HAUNTED CANADA 12

MORE FRIGHTENING TRUE TALES

JOEL A.
SUTHERLAND

Illustrations by
Steven P. Hughes

Scholastic Canada Ltd.
Toronto New York London Auckland Sydney
Mexico City New Delhi Hong Kong Buenos Aires

To all the brave souls who love a good ghost story as much as I do and dare to read on.

Scholastic Canada Ltd.
604 King Street West, Toronto, Ontario M5V 1E1, Canada

Scholastic Inc.
557 Broadway, New York, NY 10012, USA

Scholastic Australia Pty Limited
PO Box 579, Gosford, NSW 2250, Australia

Scholastic New Zealand Limited
Private Bag 94407, Botany, Manukau 2163, New Zealand

Scholastic Children's Books
1 London Bridge, London SE1 9BG, UK

www.scholastic.ca

Library and Archives Canada Cataloguing in Publication

Title: Haunted Canada 12 : more frightening true tales / Joel A. Sutherland ; illustrations by Steven P. Hughes.
Other titles: Haunted Canada twelve
Names: Sutherland, Joel A., 1980- author. | Hughes, Steven P., 1989- illustrator.
Identifiers: Canadiana (print) 2022048368X | Canadiana (ebook) 20230157777 | ISBN 9781443195812 (softcover) | ISBN 9781443195829 (EPUB)
Subjects: LCSH: Ghosts—Canada—Juvenile literature. | LCSH: Haunted places—Canada—Juvenile literature.
Classification: LCC BF1472.C3 S989 2023 | DDC j133.10971—dc23

Photos ©: Cover: © Shutterstock.com; 12: Provincial Archives of Saskatchewan; 22: Courtesy of the White Point Beach Resort; 43: From the Collection of the Oakville Historical Society; 52: Jerrye and Roy Klotz Md; 65: Canada Post © 2016; 78: Niagara Falls (Ontario) Public Library; 84: City of Victoria Archives; 90: Courtesy of Libraries and Cultural Resources Digital Collections, University of Calgary; 95: Mhsheikholeslami; 104: Courtesy of Scott Osmond/HiddenNewfoundland.ca; 117: Geological Survey of Canada/Library and Archives Canada.

Illustrations by Steven P. Hughes.

6 5 4 3 2 1 Printed in Canada 119 23 24 25 26 27

MIX
Paper from responsible sources
FSC® C103113

CONTENTS

INTRODUCTION

These stories are all true.

I've repeated that phrase countless times over the years, and yet sometimes people don't believe me.

"Buuut," they say, the word drawn out like a rubber band about to snap, "ghosts aren't real. Right?" This is sometimes followed by nervous laughter or a hopeful look in their eyes that screams, *Please, please, please don't tell me ghosts are real!*

I always give the same answer, whether it's the answer they want to hear or not. These stories are all true — very, *very* true — to the people who experienced them. In the pages that follow you'll find people's accounts of haunted homes, hotels and restaurants. You'll encounter ghosts with red eyes, ghosts with *no eyes* and ghosts covered in blood. You'll hear phantom footsteps and midnight screams and fingernails scratching the side of a sealed barrel. You'll visit a cemetery in the middle of the night, chase the sound of bells to an empty church belfry, and even attend a seance on Halloween.

Although these stories didn't happen to me, I do a lot of research to get all the facts straight and to ensure I believe each account too. Whenever possible, I interview the people who have lived the stories, which is one of the perks of the job. To hear the details of a paranormal encounter directly from the source is thrilling, creepy and just plain fun. Many people I know have shared stories with me over the years, such as my good friend and fellow author Ishta Mercurio, who you'll meet later in this book. I'm willing to bet many people you know have had a paranormal experience or two as well. Maybe — just maybe — you've seen a ghost yourself.

There aren't many things in life more entertaining than a good ghost story. So gather some friends and loved ones, read a story or two from this book together, and then share your own stories . . . if you dare.

Frightfully yours,

THE HALLOWEEN SEANCE

Selkirk, Manitoba

Don and Shelley Lugtig heard noises upstairs.

They had just bought an old Anglican rectory in Selkirk, about thirty-five kilometres north of Winnipeg. Originally built in the 1800s, the house hadn't been lived in for many years when the Lugtigs purchased it in the late 1960s. It was in terrible shape. Many windows were broken, the ceiling had collapsed in several areas, and rocks had been shoved down the drainpipes. The kitchen and an upstairs bathroom were blackened, the lasting damage of two fires years ago. Despite these challenges, the Lugtigs decided to renovate the house instead of tearing it down and building a new house in its place. They had never done that type of work before, but they were intelligent, hard-working people, and they were confident they would learn as they went.

As they worked on the house, they often brought their four daughters with them — many hands make light work — and that's when they began to hear noises upstairs. It was creepy but not too alarming — old houses tend to make odd noises — so they tried their best to shrug it off and carry on with their work.

But when they tried to sign up to have the *Winnipeg Free Press* delivered to their house, all the delivery boys refused. They wouldn't set foot near the house. It was haunted, they said, and dangerous — they'd rather turn down the assignment and risk losing their jobs than risk losing their lives. In the end, a senior member of the newspaper's leadership team had to personally deliver the paper to the Lugtigs each and every day because no one else would do it. Once again the family simply shrugged and moved on with their lives. They didn't believe in ghosts. And kids love to make up stories about the old houses in their neighbourhoods.

For some time after they moved in, other than the occasional odd sound or a weird sensation, all was quiet and calm. The Lugtigs felt reassured that they had made the right decision in buying and renovating the rectory. But then in 1981, one of Don's friends, who was a medium and tea leaf reader, expressed interest in the house and wanted to visit with a group of paranormal enthusiasts to communicate with any spirits that might linger there. And what better night for a seance in an old rectory than October 31?

Shelley was less than thrilled with the idea. Not only was she a serious skeptic, but she and Don were incredibly busy. She worked at her fabric store in the city six days a week, and Don taught at University of Winnipeg. They also both taught night classes, making for some very long days. Shelley still wasn't sold on the idea.

"They really want to have a seance on Halloween," Don said, wanting to support his friend and trying to talk his wife into it. "They'll put on the party and we won't have to do anything. They'll bring the food."

Shelley ran out of reasons to say no, so they gave Don's friend the go-ahead and the plan was set.

Halloween was always the busiest day of the year at Shelley's fabric shop, and that year was no different. People of all ages rushed in to buy supplies for last-minute costumes and alterations, emptying shelves and leaving the store looking like a bomb had gone off. By the time Shelley arrived home at 7:30 p.m. she was exhausted. Their guests had already arrived and set everything up. There were eight or ten people, more than she had expected, and they were all dressed in elaborate costumes. After a few hours of socializing and casual conversation, they got to the business at hand. To begin they wanted to get a general feel for the spirit energy in the house in an informal way. They walked around examining the Lugtigs' house, sometimes with open eyes and sometimes with them closed, their hands out and their heads tilted as if they had heard something no one else could hear. Some claimed to get vibes from another plane of existence, while others said they could feel that the dead had joined them.

Shelley wondered what they had gotten themselves into as she grew a little uncomfortable and began to regret her decision to allow them to visit.

But it was too late to change course. At midnight, the seance officially began. The group sat in a circle in the darkened living room, held hands, closed their eyes, and called out to spirits. Shelley and Don remained in the room but did not join the circle. Instead they leaned against the back wall, maintaining a comfortable distance from the others. They didn't know what to expect. But they certainly didn't believe any ghosts would appear.

Thud! Thud! Thud!

It was the sound of something coming down the stairs. Something had been summoned.

But that something turned out to be Sarah, their youngest daughter, now sixteen, and a friend pretending to be ghosts. The girls went back upstairs, laughing all the way. After a moment, the seance resumed.

Tap! Tap! Tap!

Now something was knocking on the window, knocking to come in, knocking to . . .

Once again the culprits turned out to be Sarah and her friend. They peered through the window with wide smiles and loud squeals of mischievous delight before going back into the house and heading upstairs. Some members of the group looked less than amused by the teenagers' antics. They felt the teens were mocking and ridiculing them. But soon they resumed the seance again. And this time things got spooky fast.

Shelley and Don don't recall all the details — a common aftereffect of stressful and terrifying situations — but they do remember that the group began to receive messages from beyond the grave. One spirit, communicating through one of the people in the circle, had a message for Sarah, and that sent a shiver up and down Shelley's spine. Then several people sensed that a ghost had joined them in the room. It was the spirit of an old priest who had lived in the rectory a long time ago. He said he had spent most of his afterlife in the Lugtigs' den, which used to be his office and was where he would receive members of the community.

Eventually those who had sensed and spoken with the priest informed the others that the old man had departed, and it was time for the group to go too. The guests were energized by the experience and thankful for the opportunity to hold the Halloween seance there, but the Lugtigs were exhausted and ready to put the whole thing behind them.

And they did put it behind them, not thinking about ghosts or talking about the seance for five or six years. Shelley was home alone, relaxing on the living room couch with a good book on a beautiful afternoon. Suddenly she heard something.

What was that sound? she wondered. *There's nobody here . . .*

She craned her neck and looked through the living room doorway and up the stairs. There, standing on the top step and leaning over the banister, was a teenaged girl. She was very pale and had long, curly, blond hair that cascaded over her shoulders and the old-fashioned white dress she wore. The girl looked like she had stepped out of a black-and-white photo from a long-ago time and was trying to figure out where — or more accurately, when — she was. She cupped a hand around her ear and tilted her head to the side as if straining to hear, like she was eavesdropping on Shelley.

The girl began creeping down the stairs with only the softest rustling sound, no footfalls, peering over the banister with a look of curiosity. Watching the girl, Shelley was reminded of her own daughters and the many nights when one of them had snuck out of bed to spy on the adults socializing on the main floor. And then, before Shelley could say or do anything, the girl startled, suddenly turned to look upstairs, then flowed back up to the second floor, disappearing from sight.

Shelley was frozen for a moment, wondering who the girl was. She made her way upstairs slowly and searched each of the rooms, but there was no sign of her — she was gone.

And she never came back. The fact that the house had only been inhabited by Anglican priests before the Lugtigs offered no clues as to the identity of the teenaged ghost. But seeing is believing, and although Shelley only saw the ghost once, she never forgot the experience.

THE BAD PLACE

Coalfields, Saskatchewan

It was a bad place. That's all Andy McKee's grandfather told the young boy about the patch of land between the Souris River and the bottom of the clay cliff upon which their house was perched. The house overlooked the river, giving Andy a bird's eye view of the land below. He desperately wanted to explore it, but his grandfather forbade it, simply repeating that it was a bad place.

Andy lived there with his father and grandfather. His mother and baby sister had died in childbirth when Andy was one. Theirs was a hard, tiring life. His father tried to farm the land, but the topsoil around the house was so thin that they could barely grow enough vegetables to feed themselves through the winter, let alone feed their livestock. The soil beside the river never dried out and would have been much better for crops, but the grandfather wouldn't even let his own son, a grown man, go down there. Andy's grandfather threatened to throw them out of his house if anyone tried. So Andy's father gave up on farming and worked in the local mines through the winters and on the railway through the summers. Father and son obeyed the grandfather — they avoided the bad place.

But Andy spent countless hours sitting at the top of the cliff, his legs dangling over the edge, staring at the ground below. It seemed like an unexplored paradise to his young eyes, filled with bushes ripe with sweet summer berries, colourful birds singing in the trees and fish jumping and splashing in the river. He could see nothing bad in the bad place and couldn't imagine what his grandfather was afraid of. But Andy was a little afraid of his grandfather and wouldn't dare disobey him. And so, throughout his pre-teen years, Andy sat, and he looked longingly, but he didn't dare venture down the river.

Until 1930, when Andy turned fourteen. Andy was no longer as afraid of his grandfather as he had been when he was younger. The old man was well into his seventies and both his health and his mind were beginning to fail him. He spent most his days dozing in bed or on a chair on the front porch, and he often mistook Andy for his father. One hot day in August, while his father was at work and his grandfather was asleep on the porch, Andy was struck with the conviction that he finally had to venture into the bad place. The rule was nonsensical, and he'd be there and back before his grandfather realized he'd been gone.

There was a gully a short distance along the bluff, and Andy made his way down slowly, under the intense heat of the summer sun. Insects chirped and buzzed around his head as sweat ran down the back of his neck.

As soon as Andy reached flat ground, he was filled with the unshakeable feeling that he had made a dreadful mistake. He wasn't afraid he'd get caught — he was simply afraid of the land. He instantly knew that his grandfather had been right all along, but it was too late for Andy to turn back. He began walking as if he was in a dream, a nightmare, moving him toward the river. The berries looked even more delicious up close, but he was too frightened to taste one. The squawks of birds from a nearby tree nearly scared him to death. He felt like he was being watched by some unseen presence. By the time he reached the riverbank, his shirt was plastered to his skin with sweat. But he was also so cold that his body shivered uncontrollably.

Not knowing what else to do, Andy threw a few stones into the river, then turned and headed back to the safety of his home. Although nothing bad had happened to him, he began to cry as he picked up his pace, but then he stopped dead.

There was a man standing in a patch of shadow at the foot of the cliff. He was the tallest man Andy had ever seen, and he wore a buckskin jacket and a wide-brimmed hat. His eyes looked like two black pits set deep within his stern face. He pointed at Andy as if accusing the boy of being somewhere he shouldn't be.

Andy was certain of two things: he was in the presence of a ghost, and if he stayed there any longer he would die. He ran to the gully and raced up the cliff in a panic, and as soon as he reached the top he fell to the ground in a heap, his body shivering harder than ever. He stayed there for a long time. When he was finally able to stand up, he went straight to his house, unable to cast a glance back at the bad place. He was too afraid by the prospect of what he might see, so he vowed to never return.

His grandfather was still asleep in his chair on the front porch, a small relief. Andy knew that if he had been awake, his grandfather would know that something wasn't right, and Andy didn't want to have to answer any of the old man's questions. Later in the day Andy cooked a modest meal for the two of them — his father was working a double shift and wouldn't return before the following day. After dinner Andy's grandfather read the Bible by lamplight before Andy went to bed.

As bad as the day had been, the night was much worse. The moment Andy fell asleep the nightmares began, vivid and terrifying. He was lying on the ground in the bad place, unable to move. It was unnaturally dark. Bison bellowed all around him and the night was filled with gunfire and men's screams. Warm blood splattered Andy's face, so thick and real that he could taste it. With each bang another bison hit the ground with a tremendous thud, and Andy was convinced he was going to be crushed to death.

He woke up in the middle of the night with a start, soaked in sweat. His mouth was as dry as sand, so he went to the kitchen for a glass of water, stumbling once or twice along the way. Lamplight flickered in the kitchen, and Andy was surprised to find his grandfather in the same spot where he had left him, sitting at the table with the Bible open before him. At first he thought his grandfather had fallen asleep, but his eyes were open and staring blankly at Andy. The boy reached out a trembling hand and poked his grandfather's shoulder. The old man's body tumbled off his chair and hit the ground hard.

Andy had never seen a dead body before, but he knew he was looking at one now. He dragged his grandfather into the old man's room and lifted him onto the bed. Then, not wanting to spend any more time alone with his grandfather's body, Andy got dressed and ran all the way to the mines to give his father the sad news. They drove home together in silence, put Andy's grandfather in the back of their pickup truck, and took him to the undertaker in nearby Bienfait.

Nothing went right after that. It barely snowed through the winter, and it was an unusually dry spring followed by a scorching summer. It was still next to impossible to grow any crops on their property — a hardship made harder by the Great Depression. Then, to make matters even worse, on September 29, 1931, the miners in Bienfait went on strike to improve their wages and working conditions. This led to a confrontation, later known as the Estevan Riot, between the miners and the Royal Canadian Mounted Police that resulted in the deaths of three people. Andy's dad was at the demonstrations and felt lucky to return home alive, but he was clearly at the end of a threadbare rope.

A funeral for three miners killed during the Estevan Riot, 1931

"We're going to freeze this winter if we don't do something," his father told Andy the next morning. "We're going to have to gopher out some coal."

"How can we do that?" Andy asked, dreading the answer.

"I've been mining long enough to know there's a seam of coal all the way along the Souris," his father said. "We'll gopher into the bluff below."

"You can't go down there!" Andy yelled. It was the first time he had ever raised his voice at his father. "Grandad was right! It's a bad place!"

His dad laughed, but it wasn't a happy sound. He said Andy was as superstitious as his grandfather. "But he's dead now and we can put all that nonsense behind us."

Then his dad dropped a bombshell that shocked Andy to his core. Andy's grandfather had murdered a Métis family on his property many years before and buried them in the bluff.

"It was on his conscience ever since," Andy's dad said. "That's why the old devil never let us go down."

Andy was stunned, both by his grandfather's unspeakable crime, and that his dad still wanted to go to the river despite knowing what had happened there. "I've been down there," he said. "It's haunted. It's a bad place. I won't go down again, ever."

"Please yourself, boy," his father said with a shrug. He carried his pick and shovel on his shoulder and made his way down the bluff.

Andy watched him go, helpless and overwhelmed by dread. He knew there was nothing he could do to stop him, and he was certain something bad was about to happen. He went back inside and waited for his father to return. The day felt like the longest in his life, and he had a feeling the worst was yet to come.

He returned to the cliff's edge. Night had fallen, and it was too dark to see. All was quiet and still.

"Dad?" Andy called. "Dad!"

No answer.

Andy took a deep breath and tried to steady his nerves, then made his way down to the bad place.

The bushes at the base of the cliff were crushed flat,

as was his father. His body was completely unrecognizable. It looked like he had been trampled by a ghostly herd of bison, just like in the nightmare Andy had had the night his grandfather died.

Andy picked up his father's shovel and dug a hole. Soon his muscles were sore, and he needed a short break. He looked up and saw the tall man standing in the shadows watching him. It was a chilling sight, but Andy knew that the tall man meant him no harm. Once the hole was large enough, he buried his father, threw the shovel into the bushes, climbed the bluff, and walked past the house. He didn't stop walking until he reached the city of Estevan, approximately twenty kilometres west. Andy hopped on a freight train that was bound for Toronto, and he never looked back.

Later he felt fortunate to be alive, but he often wondered if he should have been buried in the bad place too. His dreams were occasionally filled with the pounding sound of bison hooves and the stench of blood. It just shows that you can leave your home, but your home doesn't always leave you.

THE TRAILER IN THE WOODS

Peterborough, Ontario

It was almost too good to be true.

Eric and Lori had been looking to buy a vacation property they could afford for two years. The trailer in the Pigeon Lake trailer park wasn't overpriced at all. And it was perfect, with air conditioning for the summer, heating for cooler nights and a bedroom large enough to fit a king-size bed. The lot was extra large and surrounded by a dozen mature trees, providing shade and privacy for the grand deck.

So as the owners of the trailer park gave the couple a tour, Eric asked them to be honest: what was wrong with the trailer?

The owners said there was nothing wrong with it.

After a pause and a little prodding, they added that the previous owners had been a retired couple. The wife had recently died and the husband had too many happy memories connected to the property. It would be too painful for him to return. He needed to sell the trailer quickly and move on with his life.

Satisfied with that answer, Eric and Lori decided to purchase it on the spot. They moved in the following weekend.

After spending all of Saturday cleaning the trailer, setting up their things and rearranging the furniture to their liking, they relaxed on the deck with a couple of cold drinks as the sun set behind the trees. Their dog explored the area around the trailer, sniffing out a thousand appealing scents he wasn't accustomed to from his life in the city. The gentle sounds of insects buzzing and a loon calling on the lake created a peaceful soundtrack for the evening. Life was good, and Eric and Lori were pleased with their decision. They went to bed content.

Eric woke with a start at 3 a.m. There were footsteps coming from the kitchen. Lori was still sound asleep beside him. Who was in their trailer? He sat up and listened. Was it their dog, getting used to their new place?

Eric heard a cupboard door slam shut. It couldn't be the dog.

With a feeling of dread weighing heavily upon him, Eric got up. He nearly stepped on the dog, who was on the floor pressed tight against the edge of the bed, as if hiding. The dog was awake and staring intently toward the kitchen.

Eric opened the bedroom door and turned on the bathroom light. The trailer wasn't large, and he could see the kitchen and living room from where he stood. Both were empty. Perhaps the sounds he thought he had heard had come from outside the trailer, or perhaps they had been in his imagination. He entered the living room, turned on another light, and noticed that the cupboard door over the kitchen stove was wide open. He could have sworn all the cupboards had been closed when he and Lori went to bed. Had she gotten up earlier in the night for a glass of water and forgotten to close the cupboard? Or had an intruder actually been in the trailer? He looked outside but didn't see anyone in the darkness of the surrounding trees. He made sure to lock the front door, turned off the living room light, and went back to bed, leaving the bathroom light on just in case. Fortunately, he slept the rest of the night without further interruptions.

But when they returned the following weekend, the same thing happened. Footsteps in the middle of the night, cupboard doors that opened and shut on their own, and a dog that was clearly terrified from sundown to sunup. A search of the trailer revealed no one. It happened again the next few weekends too, so Eric and Lori were happy to spend the following weekend at their house in the city, where they could sleep through the night without being disturbed.

The next time they returned to the trailer a neighbour swung by. He seemed preoccupied, and then took a deep breath and said what was on his mind.

"What is going on in your trailer?" he asked in a rush.

"I don't know what you mean," Eric said.

The neighbour had seen lights flickering inside the trailer the previous weekend. When he approached to try to figure out who was inside, he heard heavy footsteps outside on the deck, followed by the sound of the sliding door opening and closing.

"No one was there!" he said

Eric looked at the trailer, wondering if they had made a grave mistake when they bought it.

Fortunately the nighttime disturbances stopped by the end of June and they didn't hear footsteps and doors and cupboards opening on their own for the rest of the summer.

It didn't last. The following May, during the Victoria Day long weekend, Eric was once again awoken by footsteps in the kitchen at 3 a.m. They were heavier than before. Lori was still asleep, but she was tossing and turning and talking in her sleep.

"Yes," she whispered. "No. No. Yes. No." It was as if someone was asking her questions.

The footsteps plodded along the hall toward the bedroom. When the footsteps stopped right outside the open door, a menacing black shadow appeared on the wall, but there was no one there.

Eric was so scared that he feared he might have a heart attack.

The dog bounded onto the bed and pointed his rigid body toward the door, growling with teeth bared and hackles raised.

The shadow slowly receded from view. Eric couldn't

believe it. The dog had scared off the terrifying presence that haunted their trailer! The dog laid down and stopped growling but kept a watchful eye on the doorway.

Lori fell silent and still too. Eric didn't know how she hadn't woken up. He expected the footsteps to return, but soon he slipped into an uneasy slumber.

The next morning, Eric filled in Lori on the night's disturbing events and asked if she knew why her sleep had been so troubled. She recalled dreaming that she was speaking with an old woman in their trailer, a woman with many questions, but she couldn't remember the specifics. *Could this be the deceased woman who had previously owned the trailer?* It seemed likely, but the thought brought no comfort.

Whoever the ghost was, they walked through the trailer at 3 a.m. each night Eric and Lori were there for the next month. Fortunately, like the previous year, the disturbances stopped at the end of June. Even more fortunate, they didn't resume the following year, or any year thereafter. The ghost had departed once and for all.

The couple came to believe that the old woman who used to own the trailer had been reunited with her husband in the afterlife, and that she was no longer tethered to this realm. Finally Eric and Lori had the peace and quiet they had always wanted during their weekend getaways. But memories linger, and every bump in the night — no matter how quiet — was accompanied by a shiver and a skipped heartbeat.

POISON IVY

Hunts Point, Nova Scotia

Wind howled and snow piled up against the walls at White Point Beach Resort when Johnny and Billy, a couple of groundskeepers, arrived for what they knew would be a tiring day at work. The resort was closed for the winter, but the driveway and paths still needed to be cleared so the owners and staff could access the building.

Johnny and Billy cleared the driveway with a truck that had a plow affixed to the front. As they approached the main lodge, they saw something they couldn't believe. The front door slowly opened and closed on its own. The building was supposed to be empty. Shocked, they parked the truck and got out for a closer look. A set of footprints in the freshly fallen snow led to the door. They opened the door and went inside where the mystery deepened. There were snowy footprints on the floor. Hoping to find a perfectly rational explanation, the two men performed a thorough search of the resort, inside and out. There was no one else there. No one living, that is.

It's no secret that the resort is haunted. A section of the company website titled "Our History" matter-of-factly states that Ivy Elliot, who ran the dining room in the late 1920s, haunts the main lodge. Some hotels and inns try to deny or cover up their haunted history, but not White Point. Its ghosts are part of the resort's DNA, thanks in part to the sheer volume of sightings that have been reported since its humble beginning in 1928 as a hunting and fishing lodge.

Ivy — the ghost most commonly seen — had a reputation for setting very high standards for her kitchen and dining room staff and insisting on perfection, earning herself the nickname Poison Ivy. Death hasn't slowed her down at all, as many staff have heard Ivy's ghost sternly call out their name when they've made a mistake at work. And when she's displeased, she makes her feelings known by flinging cooking utensils across the kitchen, lighting candles that refuse to be blown out, playing music from radios that are unplugged, and turning lights on and off.

Stephanie Miller, who used to work at the resort, would often hear Ivy's footsteps move through the dining room and pause outside her office door. Stephanie believed that Ivy was either keeping a watchful eye over her to make sure she worked hard, or that she wanted the office for herself. She also believed she once saw Ivy's ghost in the basement.

The dining room that Ivy ran at White Point Beach Resort

Bruce Clattenburg, a night engineer at the resort, saw Ivy in 2000 during a February snowstorm. It was the middle of the night and Bruce was salting the paths when a woman came around the corner of the main lodge and headed toward him. The freezing cold wind was blowing in from the Atlantic Ocean, yet the woman was only wearing a thin black coat.

"Awful cold to be out tonight," Bruce said to the woman as she passed.

She didn't stop, reply or acknowledge Bruce in any way.

Everything about her was peculiar, but Bruce still had plenty of work to do and he wanted to finish up and go inside as soon as possible. He set back to the task at hand. But then he realized that the woman hadn't left a single footprint in the fresh snow. She was still within sight, so he ran after. She disappeared when he was a little less than two metres away. She had been tall and thin with long, brown hair. She matched Ivy's description perfectly.

Sometime later on a foggy night, Bruce began talking with a couple staying at the resort who had just returned from a late walk on the beach. With a quiver of fear in their voices, they told him they had seen a man and a woman appear out of the fog and then disappear as the two couples neared one another. Bruce's theory was that the woman had been Ivy, and the man had been Danny, who used to work at the resort as a caretaker in the winter and cook in the summer. He was known to be good friends with Ivy, and after she died, he was often found speaking with someone no one else could see — when asked who was there, Danny's typical response was that Ivy had stopped by and they were having a lovely conversation. After Danny passed away, cabin 137, where he had lived, became a hotbed of paranormal activity, including flickering lights and the murphy bed lowering from the wall on its own.

And then there's the young boy, the third ghost regularly seen around the resort. One afternoon Bruce was working at the boathouse when a couple returned from a boating trip, clearly agitated about something. They had seen a young boy in overalls, about nine years old, standing on the shore of a small uninhabited island waving at them as they passed. They waved back and asked if he needed a ride to the mainland, but he didn't respond. Instead he continued to stare at the same spot and wave, as if he didn't see them at all, until their canoe drifted out of his line of sight. It was strange and unsettling. Thinking the boy must need help, they canoed to shore. But the boy had disappeared, and a search of the island turned up no trace of him.

Upon hearing this, Bruce immediately thought of a young boy matching the couple's description who had lived in the area in the 1920s. He and some friends loved playing on one of the small islands not far from the resort's beach, the same island where the couple had spotted the waving boy. One summer, when he was eight or nine years old, the boy took his raft to the island alone. He was never seen again, and his body was never discovered.

A few years later, Bruce and another staff member were pulling a boat out of the water. The work was going well until the boat suddenly stopped three metres from shore. They tugged harder on the rope. The boat didn't budge. They pulled as hard as they could but it made no difference — it was as if the boat had become encased in cement.

Laughter rang out all around them, chilling their blood. Although they couldn't see anyone, they could tell it was the laughter of a young boy.

They did their best to ignore the sound, got in a canoe, and paddled out to the boat. It must have been blocked by something underwater. The laughter grew louder. When they were halfway there, they saw a young boy dressed in overalls sitting in the boat. He was smiling and held the rope in his hands. Bruce had a sinking sensation that they were dealing with a ghost. But then the boy disappeared as suddenly as he had appeared. Bruce and his colleague couldn't believe their eyes. They paddled back to shore, got out of the canoe, and pulled the rope once more. This time the boat came in quickly without a struggle.

It seems no matter where you turn, you're bound to confront something that goes bump in the night when you stay at the White Point Beach Resort.

SPICE AND SPIRITS

Hay River, Northwest Territories

CRASH!

Linda Duford fell to the ground in fright. She stayed there for a long time, too terrified to move. The crash had come from the other side of the swinging doors in The Back Eddy Cocktail Lounge and Restaurant. Linda knew there was no one on the other side of the swinging doors.

The phantom crash — loud enough to wake the dead — was Linda's first sign that her family's restaurant, which they'd recently purchased, was haunted. It wouldn't be her last. A few years later, in 2004, Linda was working in the dining area with her parents when they all saw a blurry figure float through the restaurant. It appeared to be a man, and they had a feeling that it was one of the building's previous owners. Perhaps he had been responsible for the loud crash Linda had heard a few years before.

The restaurant's first owner and founder, chef Bill Laws, opened the establishment in 1974. It became a popular dining location famous for its proprietary Back Eddy's Seasoning. Although Bill sold the restaurant in 1987, he continues to sell the spice online to buyers around the world. When Linda's family purchased the restaurant in 2000, they thought they were taking ownership of an establishment best known for its spice, not its spirits.

Some people have reported seeing a cowboy with no feet, while others have seen misty forms as thick as clouds floating through the air.

In 2006, a Hay River man died in Fort Resolution, a small community 160 kilometres east. He was a large man, too big to fit into any of the caskets available in the community, so he was wrapped in a white sheet for the drive back to Hay River. Word of the deceased man's arrival spread through town. That night Linda and her father saw him — or rather, his ghost — appear in the front entrance of the restaurant. A moment later he was gone.

The next night, two women were enjoying a meal at a table near the bar when the lights above them started flickering as rapidly as a strobe light. Linda flicked the switch to shut off the lights for good — she could always light some candles if it was too dark — but nothing happened. The lights continued to flash. She tried the switch a few more times with no effect. It was as if the lights were possessed.

After apologizing to the women, Linda offered to move them to a different table so they wouldn't be seated directly beneath the flickering lights. They thanked her and stood to move. The flickering immediately stopped. The women sat back down, and the lights started flashing again.

The women later told Linda they were related to the man who had died in Fort Resolution, and Linda shared that she had seen his ghost the night before. Everyone agreed that turning the lights off and on was the man's way of making his presence known. Why he had chosen to haunt Back Eddy, no one could say.

In 2018 Linda and her sister sold the restaurant. Their parents had since passed away and the sisters were ready to pursue other interests. Back Eddy reopened under new management the day after Halloween, and up until her final day as co-owner, Linda always felt like she was never alone in the restaurant, even when she *was* alone. After eighteen years at the restaurant welcoming customers — both alive *and* dead — it was time to move on.

STORMY CEMETERY

Liverpool, Nova Scotia

Willie stood alone in the cemetery and wept. Wisps of fog snaked around the tombstones, obscuring the etched names and dates from view, but he knew his way around — he'd spent a good deal of time there over the years. He placed fresh flowers in the wooden vase of the grave before him, stood a little longer in silence, then made his way home slowly.

The sun set on the horizon, and in a moment the world turned dark. It started to rain. Willie began to feel a little off and, thinking he might be getting sick, picked up his pace.

The lights were on when he got home. Willie never turned them off — not earlier that day, and not ever.

Because he wasn't feeling well, he decided to skip his evening meal. He didn't bother clearing the table he had set earlier in the afternoon, which included one setting for him and one setting for *her.*

Plink, plink, plink, plink, plink! Willie listened to the rain on his roof as he lay in bed and drifted off into an uneasy sleep.

Sometime later he woke to a different sound. It was a sound he couldn't quite place. Moonlit shadows from tree branches outside his window danced on his bedroom walls like bony fingers looking to catch and claw and scratch. Willie sat up and looked at the corner of the room where he thought he'd heard the sound. His eyes slowly adjusted, and then he saw them.

There were ghosts in his room.

Many years before, as a young man fresh out of school, Willie had taken work in Boston, Massachusetts. There weren't many jobs in Nova Scotia and he thought he'd make his fortune in the United States. His major regret in leaving Canada was that he'd also left the love of his life, a kind and gentle woman named Annie. The couple planned to marry, buy a house, and start a family as soon as they could afford it, so Willie saved as much money as possible from his work as a carpenter and sent the money to Annie for safekeeping. She worked in a store in Liverpool and saved everything she could too.

Willie passed the time by writing letters to Annie, reading books and walking the streets of Boston. One evening a rose-shaped gold brooch with a diamond in the centre caught his eye, and he knew he needed to buy it for Annie, but he didn't want to spend the money he was saving for their house. So he took on a second job at night and worked long hours until he had earned enough to buy the brooch. He raced to the store afraid someone else might have already purchased it and was relieved to find the brooch still in the window waiting for him. The jeweller offered to engrave Annie's name on the back. Willie sent it to her, and she wrote back a lovely letter, ending with, "I will always treasure it."

Once they had saved enough money, Willie returned to Nova Scotia. He and Annie married and moved into their dream home. It was small and modest but everything they'd always wanted. They soon tried to have kids but weren't successful. Still, Willie and Annie were happy.

Willie's brother lived nearby, and he had a six-year-old daughter named Martha who spent plenty of time at Willie and Annie's house. The newlywed couple enjoyed their time with their niece, who added a sense of childlike whimsy to their house and enjoyed playing dress-up with her aunt's adult clothing. Life was good.

One day Annie went to get her brooch, but it wasn't where she always kept it. The only explanation the couple could think of was that Martha had taken it while she was playing with Annie's things and neglected to return it. They asked the young girl, but she couldn't remember if she had played with it, and if she had she certainly couldn't remember where she had left it. They practically tore the house apart in their search for the missing piece of beloved jewellery, growing more and more frantic and upset with every passing minute and hour and day. But their efforts were for naught. The brooch was nowhere to be found.

Willie lost control and lashed out at Annie, blaming the missing brooch on her, reminding her she had said she would always treasure it. Annie was cut deep by her husband's words, and he regretted them immediately. It was their only fight, and they carried the hurt and the shame forever.

Tragedy struck two years later. Young Martha died mysteriously after a seizure. Her untimely death reminded Willie how awful he still felt about the episode with the missing brooch. But he and Annie never spoke about the fight.

More years passed, happy years, before tragedy paid another visit to the family. Annie grew sick and was diagnosed with tuberculosis, a serious infectious disease that attacked her lungs. She clung to life for as long as possible and tried to remain upbeat, but in the end the disease beat her. When she died, Willie felt like part of his own soul had died with her.

From that day on, he never turned the lights off. He kept them on all through the night as a beacon to guide Annie home. He always set two places for every meal, believing that she would never let him eat alone. And he spent as much time as possible at her grave, placing fresh flowers in the wooden vase he'd made for her.

And then, one foggy, rainy night, the ghosts came. Willie recognized them immediately.

Annie and Martha. They stood hand in hand. Water dripped on the bedroom floor from their wet hair and faces, the sound mixing with the rain on the roof. *Plink, plink, plink, plink, plink!*

Although he had hoped Annie would return, Willie couldn't believe his own eyes.

She approached the bed quickly, a look of urgency on her face. "Willie, we have found the brooch. Martha remembered where she left it. Come!"

Annie and Martha left the room and Willie followed. They went up the stairs to the attic, Martha in the lead, and crossed to the southern corner. There was a hole in the floorboards not much larger than a dinner plate. Martha knelt and stuck her head and an arm into the hole. After a moment she stood back up and handed Willie a piece of white fabric. Willie placed it on the floor and unrolled it slowly. It was Annie's wedding veil — her long-lost brooch was in the centre.

The attic was filled with the sound of sobbing, but when Willie looked up from the brooch, he was startled to discover the ghosts were gone. He went back to his bedroom and placed the veil and brooch beneath his pillow. Sleep didn't come easily after what he had been through, which had been both a welcome and eerie experience, but eventually he drifted into a light, troubled sleep. When he woke early the next morning he wondered if it had been a dream. But when he reached a hand under his pillow, his fingers landed on the brooch.

The next few days were hot and dry, and Willie wondered if he'd ever see his dearly departed wife again now that she had helped him find the brooch. Then one night the rain returned in a downpour. At 2 a.m. Annie returned. Once again, she was soaked from head to toe and water pooled around her feet. She approached the bed with a look of desperate hope.

"Why don't you help me, Willie?" she whispered. "We have the brooch back. Let's not quarrel anymore."

Willie told her he would do anything for her and if she returned to him, he would never fight with her again. He reached out to hug her, but she backed away into the doorway.

"Come help me, Willie," she said.

Without hesitation he jumped out of bed and followed her outside into the storm. She led him to the cemetery, through the gates, straight to her grave. But before she said or did anything else, she disappeared.

"Annie!" Willie called, scanning the cemetery. "Annie!"

There was no answer.

Still, Willie continued to call her name again and again until he began to fear that someone might notice him standing alone in a cemetery in the middle of the night in the pouring rain, calling out to his dead wife, and think he had lost his mind.

Suddenly a crack of lightning lit the sky and a second later Willie had to cover his ears against a clamorous boom of thunder that shook the ground and reverberated through his skull. Terrified, Willie fled from the cemetery and raced for the safety of home.

Weeks passed and Willie grew tired and weary. He stayed awake as late as possible each night in the hope that Annie would return, but she didn't. Not until the next rainstorm.

She appeared that night and went through the same motions. Dripping wet, she pleaded for help and led Willie out into the rain and to her grave, where she disappeared. Willie remained in the cemetery for as long as he could before returning home, just as scared and confused as before.

The next night it rained again, and Annie returned. And the next night and the next.

Finally Willie had an idea what Annie might want. He walked to the cemetery early in the morning and examined the wooden vase. When he picked it up, he found the bottom was rotten and there was a small hole in the ground where the base had been. He poked a long stick into the hole and discovered it was quite deep. Every time it rained the vase must have funnelled water at that precise location, creating the deep hole, which had obviously disturbed Annie's ghost. That's why she only appeared when it rained, soaked to the bone, and led Willie to her grave.

Willie fixed the vase and filled it once more with fresh flowers. He never saw Annie again. She had given him a little peace when she and Martha led him to the missing brooch, and he in return had given her a little peace by fixing her vase. Although he was sad that he didn't see her again, he was happy that her eternal slumber was no longer disturbed by the rain.

Locked Away for Eternity

Winnipeg, Manitoba

There was something weird about the woman in the window. She was wearing an old-fashioned blouse with puffy sleeves and her hair was tied up in a bun, making her appear as if she had stepped right out of the past. She might have been an actor onsite for a film shoot, but Kristen Verin-Treusch, a tour guide who had researched the Vaughan Street Jail extensively, knew there wasn't any filming on that evening's schedule.

Kristen was standing outside the jail with her tour group, sharing some history about the building while they waited to be let in, when she spotted the woman. The woman had passed by one of the second-floor windows of the south wing, visible from the waist up. When a guard opened the door a few minutes later, the jail was as quiet as a morgue.

"How did that lady get upstairs?" Kristen asked him.

"What lady?" the guard asked, completely confused. The jail was locked up and he was alone.

Kristen finished the tour, but as soon as she was done, she investigated the second floor where she had seen the woman. It was empty, but Kristen had another concerning realization. The bottoms of the windows were as high as her shoulders. To have seen the woman from her waist up, she must have been floating half a metre above the ground. In other words, she must have been a ghost. When Kristen shared what she had experienced with others who were familiar with the jail, many admitted they too had seen a woman floating through the south wing, which used to be a women's ward.

Built in 1881, the jail held male and female prisoners — and even children as young as five — until 1930 when a new jail opened and the prisoners were transferred. It then served as a youth detention centre until 1984. Since that time, it has mostly sat empty, with only a small group of provincial employees working in an office on the main floor. The building's stern, brick facade once served as a grim warning to Winnipeg's citizens to obey the law, but it's now one of the building's greatest draws, enticing people to attend the popular tours led by Kristen and other guides. Sometimes, however, people on tour see — and hear and smell — a lot more than they had ever imagined.

Shortly before the youth detention centre closed, a

young man named Chuck heard footsteps shuffle along the corridor outside his cell, but when the sound passed his door there was no one there. The footsteps continued down the hall and into a common room. A moment later, the unseen entity lifted a card table into the air and threw it to the floor. Somehow the racket didn't wake anyone but Chuck, but he spent the rest of the night shaking in fear.

Since the jail closed, most of the reports of paranormal activity have come from people on tours. One day Kristen was sharing some of the jail's history with a group of children who were gathered around her outside. The security guard on duty asked if they wanted to have a look inside. This hadn't originally been part of the plan, and the kids were excited. Kristen led them through the building, sharing facts as they went. As soon as they arrived at the old jail cells, the lights shut off, plunging the group into darkness. Some of the children started to whimper. Others cried.

The security guard yelled for the lights to be turned back on. Whoever had turned the lights off obeyed him, but some of the children were still frightened. The guard laughed it off and said that another guard must have turned the lights off as a joke, and the group made their way back outside.

Before Kristen left, the guard confided in her that there was no one else working that day, but he had a pretty good guess who had scared the group. The jail's ghosts were to blame.

To add to the experience of Doors Open Winnipeg

tours, costumed volunteers playing the roles of prisoners, guards and other historical roles sometimes make appearances. One night, a volunteer dressed as a prisoner was locked in one of the small solitary confinement cells, where Winnipeg's most notorious criminals were once chained to the walls. During a break between tours, the volunteer called for Kristen. Her cell was filled with the strong smell of roses — not perfume, but fresh-cut flowers — and she thought she might be imagining it. Kristen inhaled deeply and was overwhelmed by the same strong scent. Despite having no discernible source and being completely out of place in the old building, the smell of roses returned during subsequent tours. Kristen eventually called upon a local psychic who claimed the roses were a gift from a spirit, happy for the company.

The ghosts of the Vaughan Street Jail are unpredictable. You never know if they're going to give you a gift or the scare of your life.

EERIE ESTATE

Oakville, Ontario

When Carol arrived to work at the Oakville Museum at Erchless Estate, the alarm panel was lit up like a Christmas tree. Lights flashed and loud beeps assaulted her ears. It was 8:15 a.m. and she was the first person to arrive, so she couldn't figure out what was to blame for the disturbance. She turned off the alarm and immediately called the security company, but as far as they could tell nothing was amiss. They had no reports that the alarm had been set off, which provided Carol with zero reassurance.

Beginning to grow a little anxious, Carol made her way deeper into the old building to investigate. As she walked through the lobby, a light fixture fell from the ceiling, missing her head by mere centimetres and scaring the living daylights out of her. It seemed like it had been a deliberate attack, but that was ridiculous.

After confirming nothing was wrong on the main level, Carol headed upstairs. As she approached the second floor, she heard a commotion. It sounded like several staff members were in the building hard at work. Carol opened the door to the office and couldn't believe her eyes.

There was no one in the room — at least, no one Carol could see — but all the office equipment was operating on its own. The photocopier was spewing paper all over the floor. Each fax machine was sending and receiving faxes one after the other. And most alarmingly, a typewriter had been turned on and was typing a string of gibberish. Carol was petrified and quickly ran back downstairs, fearful something else might fall and strike her at any moment. It no longer seemed quite so ridiculous to think that the falling light fixture had been a deliberate attack.

By the time she reached the bottom of the stairs and paused to catch her breath, the museum was quiet once more. After a moment she went back upstairs, frightened by what might await her. All the equipment was silent and still. Whatever had created the disturbance was gone.

As frightening as that experience was, it wasn't the first time Carol had been haunted at work. On busy days when she had lots to do, she would often try to avoid distractions by working in a room in the oldest part of the museum. The beautiful, bright room had belonged to a woman named Emelda Chisholm back when Erchless Estate was Emelda's family home. The room had been preserved to look like it had in the 1800s, including the original wallpaper that Emelda had selected. Carol loved working in the room even though she would often be overwhelmed with a dark, foreboding feeling in the middle of the afternoon. This feeling was immediately followed by the unshakeable conviction that someone was standing right behind her, watching her, judging her. But every time Carol spun around, there was no one there.

It's believed Emelda, who died in the building in 1951, still haunts her room today, but she's not alone. People have seen up to seven different ghosts. The Italianate-style residence was built in 1858 by Robert Kerr Chisholm. He named the home Erchless Estate, and it was located beside the Custom House, built by Robert two years prior — for fifty-five years, Robert served as Collector of Customs and Postmaster for Oakville, and it was convenient to live directly beside his office. Six generations of Chisholms lived in Erchless Estate until the house was sold to the city in the early 1980s. Before the city turned it and the Custom House into a museum, they rented out the rooms for six years. During this time, at least one tenant had a ghostly encounter around the building.

Her room had a beautiful view of the front gardens, Sixteen Mile Creek and Lake Ontario. A passionate gardener, this suited the woman perfectly. She spent a lot of time in the front yard tending to flowers and growing vegetables. One warm, sunny day, she was picking yellow beans when she sensed someone behind her. She turned and saw a woman standing in the flower garden near the wrought iron fence. The stranger's dark hair was pulled back tightly, and she wore a light summer dress. She held a basket for flower picking. The two women stared at each other in silence for a moment before the newcomer disappeared right before the tenant's eyes. Suddenly alone, the tenant couldn't believe what she had seen and wondered if there was something wrong with her. She went next door to the Custom House, which by then had opened as the first phase of the museum. She asked a few questions about the Chisholms before a staff member showed her some photographs of the family. Flipping through them, the tenant nearly screamed when her eyes met those of a woman named Rebecca Chisholm, who had died in 1865. It was the same woman she had seen in the garden.

Rebecca Chisholm

The tenant had another paranormal encounter a little later. One night she was reading in bed, when suddenly she felt the mattress bounce. There was a depression in the sheets beside her, as if someone was sitting there. She then felt invisible fingers touch her forearm, making the hairs on her arm stand on end.

When the house was officially opened as part of Oakville Museum, staff began reporting unusual activity in the building. They heard children running up and down the stairs, sometimes giggling, other times whispering, "They're coming, they're coming," to one another.

A student once had a very similar experience to that of Carol in Emelda's room. She was creating a slide presentation when, in the middle of the afternoon, she was overcome by a foreboding, dark, depressing feeling. There was no one there with her and she didn't know what had caused the feeling, but she did know that she needed to get out of the room without a moment's delay.

At least two of the museum's ghosts have been captured in photographs. One was a mysterious figure who turned up in a wedding photo, and the second was a woman wearing a black dress pulling back the drapes and peering out of a second-floor window. There was no one in the museum at the time the photograph was taken.

During a Monday meeting when the museum was closed to the public, staff saw a tall, shadowy man wearing a long coat pass by the open door . . . then straight through a wall.

Late one night, the museum's handyman saw this same ghost. The handyman was alone, painting a room on the second floor while pale blue moonlight filtered in through the windows. Suddenly, the peace and quiet was broken by the sound of people talking on the main floor, followed by footsteps coming up the stairs. He didn't think too much about the sounds, assuming some staff had returned to the museum to collect their belongings. He continued to paint while he waited to see who came up . . . but no one did. With every passing second, the handyman's unease increased. Eventually he couldn't take it any longer, so he left the room. But he didn't see a soul. With a shrug, he returned to his work. A short while later he heard footsteps on the stairs again. Without wasting a moment, he ran out of the room and looked over the railing. He caught sight of a shadowy man walking through the hall on the first floor. The handyman called out, but the man didn't respond. Instead, he disappeared. Feeling far too uncomfortable to continue working that night, the handyman quickly locked up and left the building. He felt the ghost's presence had been some sort of warning from beyond telling him to leave. Like many before him, he was only too happy to comply.

History comes alive at the Oakville Museum at Erchless Estate. If only some of its history would stay dead.

THE UNKILLABLE CAT

Breckenridge, Quebec

The year was 1866 and Joe Herrington lived alone in an old log house deep in the dark woods of Breckenridge. The families in nearby farmhouses couldn't understand how he could live in that particular house alone. It had a reputation for being haunted, a reputation maintained by Joe himself. He would loudly proclaim to all who would listen that he felt like the ghosts were making him lose his mind. But he was very proud of his house and didn't want to leave.

Each and every night, after he had gone upstairs to bed and started to drift to sleep, Joe was woken by disturbing and unexplainable sounds coming from the main floor. Footsteps and moans and hisses and laughter and bangs. The phantom sounds made his stomach churn and prickled his skin with goosebumps. He never caught sight of anyone or anything when he went to investigate, so he eventually stopped going downstairs when he heard a commotion. Instead, he was happier to stay in bed, where he felt relatively safe with the sheets pulled up to his chin.

It wasn't just the sounds that scared Joe, but the damage the spirits were inflicting on his beloved house. One night he heard a mighty crash. When he went downstairs in the morning, he discovered that all his dishes had been thrown off the hutch and broken into hundreds of pieces. Another morning, after listening to a chorus of howls and screams through the night, Joe went downstairs to find all the clothing he had hung up to dry had been ripped into tiny pieces and scattered around the kitchen.

The ghosts were getting destructive, and as much as he hated being run out of his own house by forces he couldn't even see, Joe finally decided enough was enough. He moved far away from Breckenridge, never to return to that part of the province.

After everything Joe had reported, no one was brave enough to move into the log house, and it sat empty for a long time. But the house was far from quiet, for the ghosts hadn't left with Joe and they weren't shy in making their presence known. As people travelled on foot or on horseback through the woods at night, they saw lights flickering through the trees. When they approached for a closer look, they discovered the lights were coming from inside Joe's abandoned log house. Others heard the awful racket of chains being dragged across the wooden floorboards and pots and pans banging together.

Word of the haunted house spread far and wide, carried on the backs of the tales people shared with everyone they met during their travels. It became known as the most famous haunted house in the whole region. Soon, instead of avoiding it, people were visiting the house in hopes of seeing the lights and hearing the sounds.

Then a new phenomenon began to occur, but only at night. A large black cat was spotted in the windows. One passerby took the cat's sudden appearance as a bad omen and fired his rifle at the animal. That's when the strangest thing happened — the cat vanished before the bullet struck it. Odder still, the cat reappeared in a different window. The man shot at the cat a second time and a third with the same result. What he was seeing was impossible. Cats couldn't simply disappear one moment and reappear the next. The cat clearly wasn't of this world. Everyone who saw it agreed: it was a ghost.

News of the ghost cat of Breckenridge spread like wildfire. Soon there weren't only ghost hunters and thrill-seekers making the nightly pilgrimage to Joe Herrington's abandoned house, but skilled marksmen who wanted to be the first person to hit the unkillable cat. But no one was ever successful.

The cat seemed bored by the futile attempts to kill it, often looking at its attempted murderers with disdain, other times not even bothering to pay them any attention and opting to lick its paws instead.

This went on for years until, one day, it stopped without explanation. The ghost cat vanished for good, never to return, and the flashing lights and unusual sounds ceased as well.

Some cats have nine lives. Others can never die.

SPEND A NIGHT WITH THE DEAD

Qualicum Beach, British Columbia

It was autumn 1988 and the town of Qualicum Beach on Vancouver Island was aglow with the vibrant reds, oranges and yellows of fall leaves. The ocean air was crisp and cool. Shadows grew longer as the days grew shorter. A man had travelled to the town with a group of friends to see one of their favourite musicians. The musician was performing at the Qualicum Heritage Inn, so the group of friends rented rooms. The man was fortunate to get the last room available, but little did he know that Room 453 was often only filled when all other rooms were already booked. Had he known the history of the room and what other guests had experienced, he likely would have been far less thrilled.

The musician played late into the night and the friends stumbled, tired but happy, back to their rooms. The man locked his door and collapsed into bed, falling asleep shortly after his head hit the pillow. When the sun rose, he was hungry but still too tired to get up, so he decided he'd skip breakfast and remain in bed a little longer.

But then he heard his door open. His locked door. Footsteps slowly approached the bed. He was too afraid to roll over to face the intruder. Suddenly his blankets were yanked free and thrown across the room.

"Get down to breakfast!" a man's voice barked.

The man rolled over in terror, but his room was empty. The door was closed. Other than the blankets piled on the floor and the ringing in the man's ears from the intruder's voice, there was no sign anyone had been there. He got dressed in record time and raced down to the dining room for breakfast.

The Tudor-style building was originally Qualicum College, an all-boys school built in 1937. Many of the school's faculty and staff worked there for most of their careers before the school closed in 1970. One such person was Bert James, a loyal and hard-working groundskeeper who lived in a small room on the fourth floor of the college.

One spring day in the late 1960s, Bert didn't appear for breakfast. That was unlike him, as he had a habit of rising early for a quick meal before getting to work. Perhaps he had risen earlier than usual and was already working somewhere on the grounds. But later Bert wasn't present for lunch either. Alec Trumper, a janitor, decided to check Bert's room just in case he wasn't feeling well and needed some help.

Alec knocked on the door. There was no answer. He called Bert's name. Still no answer. He tried the handle. It was locked. So Alec used a screwdriver to open the door. Although he had feared the worst, he wasn't prepared for the sight that met his eyes. He found Bert lying face up on his bed, his arms raised up above his head as if reaching for the headboard. He was dead, and he didn't look at peace, which led Alec to assume he had died suddenly, perhaps painfully.

After the college closed and the building was remodelled to become the Qualicum Heritage Inn, Bert's room was converted into a guest room and given the number 453.

The Qualicum Heritage Inn in 2008

The man who'd been ordered to breakfast shared his hair-raising experience with hotel staff. They all had a feeling they knew who the ghost had been — Bert James.

Guests staying on the fourth floor regularly heard loud footsteps walking up and down the empty hall in the middle of the night. And cleaning staff often found that the furniture had been moved and the bed was messed up, even after nights when no one had slept there.

Another guest had a strange experience at the inn the same year. Devon Andrew and her husband, Adrian, were in Qualicum Beach for work. The Qualicum Heritage Inn was their favourite place to stay during visits to the area. They went to bed at 11 p.m. after a long day, but Devon woke up a short while later. Her husband, she was concerned to discover, was missing. Where had he gone so late? Devon got out of bed and began roaming the halls in search of him. She checked the stairwells, common areas and even the roof, but there was no sign of Adrian.

Then as she was searching the fourth floor, a door to her left slowly creaked open. It was 453. There was a woman standing in the doorway, staring at Devon silently. Devon peered around the somewhat strange woman into the room hoping for some clue that might lead her to her missing husband. The room was old and small, with a sloped ceiling and a small bed against a wall. Opposite the bed was a sink and mirror, as well as the bathroom door. There was no sign of Adrian. The woman who had opened the door seemed angry and hostile, which was understandable after being woken in the middle of the night, so Devon hurriedly moved along.

By 3 a.m., Devon lingered in the lobby, more scared for Adrian's safety than ever. But then . . . she slowly woke up. It had all been a dream! Her husband was standing in front of her, calling her name and looking a little concerned. She was in the hotel lobby, just like in her dream, so Devon realized she must have been sleepwalking, a fact that the hotel staff confirmed. They had called Adrian once they realized which room Devon was staying in. Adrian apologized and quickly led his wife back to their room.

The next morning, feeling embarrassed, Devon and Adrian asked to speak to a manager to apologize for the disturbance. Hotel executive Linda Bishop met the couple and listened with interest as Devon described her dream. Curious, Linda asked if Devon could retrace her sleep-walking steps. Devon led Linda to the fourth floor and stopped outside the door the woman had opened. It was closed, but there were no numbers on it. Linda explained that, for some unknown reason, the numbers had a habit of falling off the door, and they hadn't been replaced yet since no one was currently staying in the room. Eerily, Devon correctly identified the room's number, which she had seen in her dream.

"Let me tell you the layout of the room," Devon said before they entered. She then described the interior of the room in detail, including the small bed, the sink, and the unique sloped ceiling.

Linda unlocked and opened the door. The room matched Devon's description, tiny detail by tiny detail. No one could figure out how that was possible. The room hadn't been booked the night before. So who was the woman Devon had seen while sleepwalking, and how did Devon know what it looked like from the inside? Linda informed Devon and Adrian that the room was known by hotel staff as the "ghost room," thanks to the many experiences guests and staff alike had reported over the years. Did the room serve as a conduit for spirit energy due to the ghost of Bert James residing there for eternity?

Whatever the cause, the fourth floor has no shortage of haunts. In the spring of 1999, mother and son Ruth and Michael Hutchinson booked separate rooms on that level, and Ruth had a very distressing stay. It was afternoon and Ruth was reading a book in bed, when she heard the muffled sound of a boy crying coming from the room next to hers. It sounded like he was in physical pain, and as Ruth listened his wailing grew louder. Soon other voices could be heard too, particularly an older woman who seemed to be trying her best to calm the young boy. This went on for more than five minutes, at which point Ruth felt she should do something and stepped into the hall. But the moment she left her room, the sounds stopped abruptly, and she couldn't hear them when she returned.

Although something about the voices gave her the creeps, Ruth returned to her bed and her book. But as soon as she resumed reading, she heard chanting coming from the room next door. The rhythmic chanting wasn't in a language Ruth recognized, and as she listened the voices grew louder and louder. The chanting frightened her — it sounded otherworldly. She put her ear to the wall, and the chanting stopped immediately.

Ruth turned on the television to fill her room with sounds she could understand, then turned on all the lights. She had wanted to take a shower but decided not to — she felt like an unseen presence had entered her room and was watching her. As she was getting ready to leave the next morning she heard a loud moan — not from another room, but from the middle of her own. Terrified, she was very relieved when she met up with her son in the hallway a little later. After telling him what had happened, he admitted he had heard footsteps and doors slamming during previous stays. Shortly after, a couple of cleaning staff told her that no one was staying in the room beside hers. They also shared that other guests had heard piano music and singing coming from that same room in the past. At least she wasn't the only person who had heard the ghosts. Far from it.

Based on these experiences and countless others, it seems like some nights there were more ghosts than guests in the Qualicum Heritage Inn.

EYES LIKE EMBERS

St. John's, Newfoundland and Labrador

It was the mid-1800s and a couple was out for a relaxing evening stroll. They walked throughout downtown St. John's greeting those they passed, stopping occasionally to gaze through shop windows, and engaged in amiable conversation. The sun was just beginning to set as they turned onto Springdale Street, but it was still pleasantly warm. The couple had no destination in mind and were content to be led by their whims, which happened to take them through a deserted field.

The woman began to shiver. Slightly at first, as if she'd caught a chill, but soon she was shaking uncontrollably. The cold penetrated deep into her bones, and yet the man felt just as warm as before. She asked him to take her home immediately as she was beginning to feel ill. Concerned for her wellbeing and wondering what could have possibly come over her so suddenly, the man agreed. They turned to leave but were stopped by an odd sight.

A short distance away, an old woman wearing a knit shawl was perched on a rock. She held a jug from which she drank deeply. The couple instantly sensed something off about her, like she wasn't real. The old woman rose to her feet and took a threatening step forward, staring at them intently. As she did so, her hair stood up around her head as if charged by electricity and her eyes turned bright red like a pair of glowing embers.

The couple ran screaming from the field and didn't stop until they were a safe distance away. Although the old woman hadn't followed them, they knew who she was. It was Alice Janes, a woman well known in that part of St. John's. But how could that be? Alice had died approximately a year before. The couple realized they hadn't seen Alice — they had seen her ghost.

Word of their encounter spread throughout the city, and it was soon pointed out that Alice hadn't died "approximately" a year before. She had died exactly a year before. Alice had risen on the first anniversary of her death. No one was surprised that Alice's ghost had remained in that empty lot on Springdale Street.

Horseracing was one of the most popular sports in St. John's throughout the nineteenth century. The St. John's Turf Club was formed in 1833 and established a small racetrack on Springdale Street that same year. The organization renamed itself the Harbour Grace Turf Club in the mid-1800s, and the Springdale Street racetrack closed in favour of a new track. But before the move, the Springdale Street track was the site a tragic event.

Alice Janes adored horseracing more than anything and was a fixture at the track. She always wore a knit shawl and never went anywhere without her jug of home-brew. During one of the races, she suffered a massive heart attack and died instantly, much to the shock and horror of the surrounding spectators. There was a large turnout at her funeral, and she was buried in a respectable location in the Anglican Cathedral of St. John the Baptist's churchyard.

She had been well-liked, a friendly soul. No one could understand why her spirit had been so angry and frightening, chasing the couple out of the lot where her beloved racetrack had once stood.

The answer was discovered the day following Alice's ghostly appearance. Several townsfolk gathered in the churchyard to offer their respects to Alice and to pray that her troubled spirit would rest in peace. They were shocked to discover her tombstone was missing. A search of the grounds was conducted, but they couldn't find it anywhere. The group was certain this explained why she had returned and why she was so angry.

For the next ten years Alice appeared on the anniversary of her death and scared the living daylights out of everyone who crossed paths with her. The locals quickly learned to avoid Springdale Street on the day she had died, but visitors had no idea who or what the creature was that chased them through the night.

Finally, a caretaker stumbled upon Alice's tombstone in a seldom-used corner of the church and returned it to her plot. Alice could finally rest in peace, and her ghost wasn't seen again.

FOR WHOM THE DEATH BELL TOLLS

Charlottetown, Prince Edward Island

DING!

The sound of a bell made Captain Cross pause as he walked into town early on the morning of October 7, 1853.

That's peculiar, the captain thought. The sound had come from downtown Charlottetown, and it was the unmistakable tinny sound of a ship bell — a sound the captain was very familiar with.

He heard it ring two more times. The captain now found it to be an ominous sound, one that filled his heart with dread. He made his way past the harbour, thinking he might be mistaken about the direction of the sound and concerned a ship might be in danger. But when he scanned the bay, he saw nothing amiss. A few ships were docked, including *The Fairy Queen*, which was to set sail for Pictou later that day.

After the bell rang two more times, the captain thought it might have come from St. James Presbyterian Church, a short distance ahead. He crossed the street, rounded a corner, and walked along Fitzroy Street toward the church. Its tall belfry loomed ahead.

The bell rang a sixth time as the captain approached the church and spotted three women, dressed all in white, through an open door. They seemed to be completely unaware of the captain's presence.

When the bell rang again it was so loud it seemed to pierce his skull. He quickly looked up at the belfry. Through the louvers, small openings that let the sound out, he thought he could see a fourth woman in white ringing the bell. When he lowered his gaze back to ground level, the door closed on its own, hiding the first three women from view.

As the captain reached the doors, the church sexton, Davy Nicholson, joined him. Davy had no idea who the women might be or why one was ringing the church bell. The pair tried to enter. But the door was locked. Through a window they could see the women climbing the stairs to the belfry. Davy went to get his keys while Captain Cross listened to the muffled sound of voices and footsteps moving up through the belfry. Davy returned a moment later accompanied by Reverend William Snodgrass. The trio unlocked the door and rushed up the tower in pursuit of the mysterious intruders.

DING!

The bell rang for an eighth time, the sound reverberating off the walls and rattling the captain's head again. He paused briefly for the sound to subside slightly, then continued. Davy threw open the hatch to the belfry at the top of the stairs.

The bell was still vibrating, but there was no one there. Not a soul. They looked through the louvers fearing that the women had jumped, but there was no one on the grounds. The women had disappeared.

The three men went back down and searched the church but still didn't find any trace of the women. The minister thought that the wind might be to blame for ringing the bell and doubted that Captain Cross and sexton Davy had seen anyone, but the captain had no doubt about what he had heard — and seen. There was nothing else to be done, so they locked the door and went about their business. The sexton and minister returned to the comfort of their homes while the captain retrieved his horse. The bell did not ring under such mysterious circumstances again and the women were never seen from that day on.

But the following day, tragic news reached Charlottetown from neighbouring towns where passengers and crew had washed ashore during the early hours of the morning. *The Fairy Queen*, one of the steamboats Captain Cross had spotted in the harbour the previous day, had broken apart and sunk in the Northumberland Strait.

As more information was revealed the story became more tragic. Over the course of the six years it had sailed, *The Fairy Queen*, a mail and passenger ship, had been battered and damaged from countless storms. Some said the engine had been replaced with that of a much older ship, and recently it had run aground on the coast near Shediac, New Brunswick. A fresh coat of paint had been applied to its hull to make it appear like it was in better shape than it was, and it passed inspection and was approved to sail. There were twenty-six people on board — thirteen crew members and thirteen passengers. A storm began to brew, not large enough to sink a seaworthy ship but strong enough to damage *The Fairy Queen* and cause it to sink. For some unknown reason, the captain and many members of the crew didn't allow the passengers to board the lifeboats. Because of this, seven people died — three men and four women.

Of the four women, three were from Charlottetown. Not only that, but they were members of St. James Presbyterian Church. Could it be that they were the three women Captain Cross and sexton Davy spotted in the church the morning before they died? And could the fourth woman spotted at the top of the belfry have been the other woman who died?

When the story of the bell ringers spread, people in town believed that the four women in white were forerunners. A forerunner can come in many forms, including the ghost of someone who is about to die. Their appearance is often seen as an ominous warning, perhaps a cry for help, and people who appear as forerunners typically die under tragic or suspicious circumstances. This could certainly be said for the four women who died when *The Fairy Queen* sank the evening of October 7, 1853. And it could be that they rang the bell eight times to mark the seven people who were about to die, plus one final ring for the ship. It would also explain why the bell sounded like it belonged to a ship, not a church.

The story has grown and changed over the years, creating a few different tellings of it, each of them equally fascinating. To this day, staff at the church receive calls from all around the world asking about the tragedy of *The Fairy Queen* and the phantom bellringers. It's a story that, just like ghosts, will never die.

Canada Post's "The Phantom Bell Ringers" stamp

SHE FOLLOWS

Sussex and Hampton, New Brunswick

Diane Hodgin was relaxing in her apartment one October day when a decorative brass bell mounted on the wall in the hallway rang frantically. She went to see what all the commotion was about, but there was no one there.

The bell rang again.

Then the hall doors slammed shut and swung open on their own.

It was clear to Diane that her apartment was haunted, and it was equally clear who the ghost was. Diane and her family had lived in the apartment building on Essex Street for many years, and they loved it there. So too did an elderly woman named Mrs. King who had lived in one of the other apartments before her death in 1989. Diane had a feeling that the commotion was Mrs. King's way of announcing she hadn't left the building, nor would she any time soon.

Later that year, every bloom was mysteriously ripped off Diane's Christmas cactus for no apparent reason, so she assumed Mrs. King was to blame. Then the pervasive smell of lavender — Mrs. King's favourite scent — began to fill the family's dining room. And doors swung open and slammed shut at all hours of the day and night. Diane, her husband and their children became accustomed to the ghostly disturbances. The family chalked it up to Mrs. King not wanting to be ignored — she seemed to like the attention, or at the very least she wanted her presence to be noted. In a manner of speaking, she became a part of the household, always there, never forgotten.

A few years later, Diane and her family had a new house built forty kilometres southwest, in Hampton, and moved out of their apartment in Sussex. A young couple, the landlord's daughter and her husband, moved in, but Mrs. King . . . she stayed put.

A year later Diane and her husband were visiting friends in their old building when she happened to bump into the landlord. As they chatted, Diane got the impression something was on his mind. Soon he revealed what was bothering him.

"I wish you would take Mrs. King with you," he said.

This caught Diane off guard, so he explained that his daughter had been living in fear for the past year. The ghost of Mrs. King scared the living daylights out of her. She was on the verge of a breakdown. Out of compassion,

Diane agreed to talk with her.

She visited the apartment and told the landlord's daughter that Mrs. King was harmless and that her presence was nothing to be afraid of. But nothing she said provided the young woman any comfort. Like the Hodgins, the young couple was planning on building their own house so they could get out of the haunted apartment, but the woman doubted she'd be able to stay there until their new house was ready. Was there anything Diane could do?

Diane saw the desperation in the woman's eyes and heard it in her voice. She suggested that she could invite the ghost to leave Sussex and move in with her family in Hampton. Would it work? Unlikely. But Diane didn't let the landlord's daughter know she had doubts. If it gave the woman a little peace of mind — even if only for a day or two until Mrs. King made her presence known again — that would be a positive thing.

Diane entered the dining room and said, "Why don't you come home with us, Mrs. King?"

Nothing happened.

But it didn't matter. The young woman was ecstatic. She thanked Diane profusely. Diane felt like the woman had simply tricked herself into believing it had worked and Mrs. King would bother her no more. Diane said goodbye and went on her way.

The following night, back in their Hampton home, Diane was relaxing in her living room with her husband, kids and their cats.

CRASH!

Everyone in the house — humans and felines alike — jumped in the air. The ear-splitting racket had come from one of the bedrooms on the second floor. The family raced upstairs to see what had happened.

Diane's son kept an old ice cream container full of marbles on the dresser in his room. It had been thrown to the centre of the room, and the marbles had rolled every which way. They had never experienced anything like that in the house.

Diane and her husband shared a troubled look.

"Mrs. King," she said.

He raised his eyebrows knowingly.

In the days that followed, doors opened and closed on their own and the dining room smelled strongly of lavender. The children had forgotten what it was like to live with a ghost, and they weren't thrilled to be haunted once more.

One day Diane's son came charging up to her, shaking with anger. "She touched me!" he yelled. "I hate that!"

Her husband was touched by Mrs. King too. He was walking along the hall one afternoon when someone suddenly pushed up against him from behind and flew past. He spun around but didn't see anyone. He entered the kitchen and spotted his wife.

"Did you just walk by me?" he asked.

She shook her head and informed him that she had been in the kitchen for half an hour.

"Mrs. King?" he asked in disbelief. Then, with a sigh, he answered his own question. "Mrs. King."

As unsettling as Mrs. King's presence was, the

scariest was yet to come. One day Diane returned home alone. As soon as she entered, she came face to face with a man blocking her way. Well, "face to face" might not be completely accurate, since she couldn't see his. Although his body was clearly visible, his entire head was surrounded by thick mist. After a few tense seconds, the man disappeared.

Diane believed Mrs. King had invited the other spirit into the home to keep her company. She clearly craved attention. The question that haunts the Hodgin family is how many more ghosts might visit their home, all because they invited Mrs. King to come live — in a manner of speaking — with them?

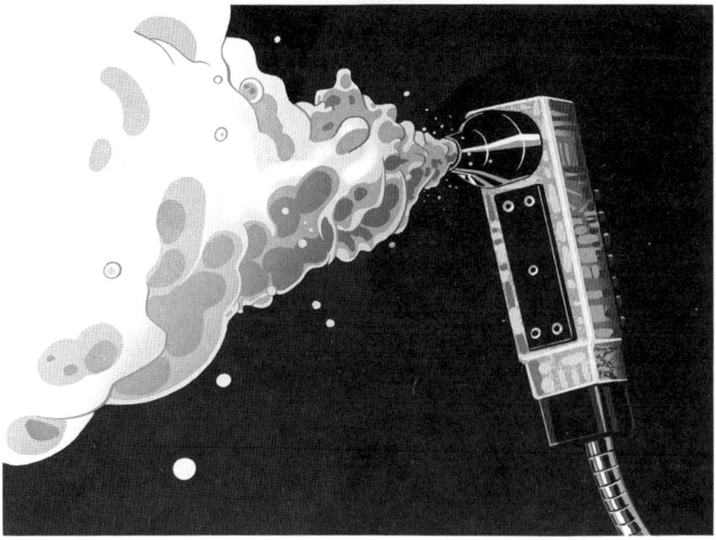

NIGHT PRANKS

Dawson City, Yukon

It was the end of the night. Lee Kirby was closing the cash register in the lounge on the second floor of the Westmark Inn Dawson City. He was all alone. The hotel was silent and calm. Suddenly the soda gun turned on right in front of him, spraying everywhere.

Lee jumped and quickly pressed a button on the gun to get it to stop. He had only worked there for a week, but he was certain he had just met the hotel's resident ghost, Kate.

He'd been warned about her the moment he arrived in Dawson City and started his new job as the manager of the hotel's two dining locations, the Keno Lounge and Belinda's Dining Room. The ghost spent most of her afterlife haunting the second floor near a room called Kate's Suite. It was said Kate died on the property many years before, but Lee didn't believe the tales. He didn't believe in ghosts at all. So he put everything he'd been told out of mind. But with each passing day he found it harder and harder to ignore the signs that the stories held more fact than fiction.

He often had an odd feeling as he walked past doorways, thinking he had seen someone in empty rooms. Window blinds moved on their own with no sign of a draft. And the incident with the soda gun wasn't an isolated occurrence. It happened a few more times — always late at night, and always when Lee was alone.

Finally, he gave in and talked with Kate, even though he couldn't see her. Maybe, he thought, that would get her to stop messing around and leave him alone.

He thought wrong. If anything, it only made her more active. One night he was in a bad mood when the soda gun started spraying, so he yelled at her to stop. It turned off immediately and Lee felt a strong gust of icy-cold wind rush past him. He knew Kate had flown out of the room, upset by the tone he had taken with her.

Lee hoped that would be the end of it so that he'd finally have a little peace. But a few nights later, as he was alone and closing the cash register, there was a bang behind him loud enough to wake the dead. He jumped out of his chair and turned around but saw nothing amiss. Once his heart had stopped pounding, he turned back to his work. Something banged on the wall again. He turned around in time to see a mirror fly off the wall, strike a table, rebound back to the wall, and crash to the floor. Miraculously, the mirror didn't shatter.

The next day, a member of the maintenance staff questioned Lee's account of what had happened, insisting that there was no way the mirror could have done what he said without breaking. Lee couldn't explain it either — if he hadn't seen it with his own eyes, he would have doubted it too. The fact was it had happened, and he knew Kate had been responsible.

Kate continued to haunt the hotel for years, making her presence known and terrifying staff and guests. Sometimes her presence was welcomed, such as one night when a group of tourists from the Atlantic provinces had taken over the lounge, eating, drinking and singing songs from home. Everyone was seated in a wide circle around a table. While most people held their drinks, one person had set their wineglass on the table. They began singing an Irish tune, and when they reached the chorus, the glass exploded, spraying the group with wine. There was a moment of stunned silence before the tourists erupted into cheers and applause, then raised their glasses (except for the person who was suddenly without one) and gave a hearty toast to Kate in thanks for joining them. Lee assumed Kate must have loved their song and couldn't contain her excitement, causing the glass to explode.

Sometime later the hotel's offices were moved from the first floor to the second, and for some reason Kate didn't seem pleased by the change. Lee and the rest of the staff thought this was because she spent most of her time on the second floor and didn't appreciate the extra hustle and bustle that had suddenly invaded her space. When the hotel's maintenance engineer stayed in one of the second-floor rooms for a brief stint, his television would often turn on, and the taps in the washroom would start blasting water. Kate also tossed his keys and other small items to the floor.

Although little is known about Kate, it's clear she craves constant attention and goes about getting it the wrong way. Although, when it comes to ghosts, many would argue that there's no *right* way — but that won't ever stop Kate from playing nighttime pranks in the Westmark Inn.

OVER THE FALLS

Niagara Falls, Ontario

A young man was locking up at IMAX Niagara after all the customers and staff had left. Although he had worked at the theatre long enough to be entrusted with this responsibility, he hadn't ever been nervous when alone in the pyramid-shaped building. But things were different that night. He felt scared and apprehensive, but he couldn't say why. Something about the dark — it made him feel unnaturally jumpy and disturbed. It was as if something was hiding in the shadows. Something waiting. Something watching.

He picked up his pace, eager to leave and get safely home, trying not to think of the ghost stories associated with the theatre that he had been told. As he passed through the gift shop, something unexpected made him stop dead in his tracks, raising the hair on the back of his neck. Down the hall, in the Daredevil Gallery, a spotlight had been turned on. But he had turned all the gallery lights off just a moment before.

Knowing he needed to investigate, despite that being the last thing he wanted to do, the man took a deep breath and started walking down the hall. The light was focused on one artifact — a massive wood and steel barrel more than three metres long and weighing nearly one ton. He took a few tentative steps toward the barrel before an ear-splitting scream cut through the silence and echoed throughout the building. It was followed immediately by the chilling sound of fingernails frantically scratching wood. The man wanted to run away but was frozen with fear, unable to move a muscle. He shut his eyes, clenched his fists, and waited for the worst to happen.

The scratching sound faded away and the light in the Daredevil Gallery slowly went out. The building was once again quiet and dark. The man left and locked the front door as quick as he could, not daring to look back as he put the theatre behind him. The stories were true. The theatre was haunted. The experience had left him traumatized. He soon quit his job, unable to spend another day in such a heightened state of perpetual fear of his workplace.

The details of that young man's experience are consistent with reports from other staff, and paint a clear picture of who haunts the theatre. The barrel that was illuminated in the Daredevil Gallery belonged to George

Stathakis. It was a barrel that became his tomb.

On Saturday, July 5, 1930, George was sealed inside the barrel so he could travel over Horseshoe Falls, Canada's tallest waterfall and the largest of the three waterfalls that collectively form Niagara Falls. But he wasn't going alone — his pet turtle, Sonny Boy, was making the trip with him. George claimed the reptile was more than 150 years old and was the bodily form of a mysterious and obscure god. As a self-proclaimed mystic and philosopher, George had announced that he was going over the falls in search of enlightenment and truth. According to official records, he was born in 1884. But he believed he had been alive for more than one thousand years and had visited Niagara Falls before it had been formed.

With a large crowd of onlookers and a crew filming the stunt, George and Sonny Boy's barrel was released from the riverbank at 2:30 p.m. and raced toward the falls. His barrel plunged over the edge to a chorus of gasps from the crowd and disappeared. It became trapped at the base of the falls for eighteen hours, under the crushing weight of the falling water. It was found at dusk the following day near the Falls View Bridge and was opened before a second crowd of curiosity-seekers. No one expected to find George alive, but the sight that met them was more chilling than anyone had anticipated. His eyes and mouth were wide, as if he had died screaming, and there were signs that he had tried to scratch his way out of the barrel. The cause of death was ruled as suffocation. Shockingly, George's turtle was still alive, and this discovery was met with applause and cheers from the crowd. George built the barrel so large it would protect him from harm, but it's believed that the barrel's weight was what trapped it behind the falls.

The barrel of George Strathaki on the morning after his fatal trip, July 5, 1930

A newspaper article that covered George's death included a quote he had given sometime before his ill-fated stunt. It was darkly prophetic: "O divine Niagara, be prepared on July the 5th to receive a faithful worshiper of your beauty and of the mystery that covers you, and if you will to keep me with you eternally as your prisoner, I accept the sacrifice in the hope that your divine nymphs will spray my grave with flowers from the gardens of your palaces."

Whether or not George's grave was covered in flowers by the falls' nymphs cannot be said, but there were plenty of signs in the IMAX Theatre indicating that his soul was unable to leave this world.

One night a projectionist thought he was alone in the booth when he spotted someone lurking in the shadows behind the large projector. Assuming it was a co-worker, he walked around to see who was there. But whoever it was had disappeared. The projectionist had felt a presence in the booth and heard noises before, but this was the first time he had caught sight of the ghost, and he was convinced it had been George.

Nighttime was when George was most active. Staff heard his footsteps plodding through the building, and he knocked over displays and tossed items off shelves in the gift shop. People reported feeling a negative energy around his barrel in the Daredevil Gallery and heard the desperate scratching of fingernails coming from within. One man once heard a voice calling from the gallery after everyone else had left for the night. Thinking a colleague had returned or a guest hadn't left at closing time, he went to investigate. As he approached the gallery, he grew more and more nervous. He slowed down, no longer sure he wanted to proceed. As he neared the gallery, he realized whoever was talking was speaking in a language he didn't understand. In a panic, he seriously considered fleeing from the building and locking whoever was in the gallery inside alone, but he carried on. As soon as he entered the gallery, the voice fell silent. The room was completely empty.

Must be George acting up, the man thought to himself, relieved he hadn't come face to face with the ghost.

The IMAX Theatre closed and sat abandoned for many years, looking more haunted than ever. Panels fell off the siding and the cracked-pavement parking lot filled with garbage and weeds. In May 2022, the building was demolished to make way for the construction of a new hotel. When construction is complete, will George wander the halls of the new building? Only time will tell, but if you ever stay there, don't be surprised if you hear the sound of fingernails scratching on wood in the middle of the night.

CREEPY CAMPUS

Victoria, British Columbia

It was a little past 9 p.m. and Linda, an instructor at Camosun College, was alone in the Young Building. She was working late and eager to leave. The old, stately building, with its long corridors and tall watchtower, was imposing, dark and more than a little creepy. Linda finished her work and was ready to print. Unfortunately, the printer on the first floor didn't work, so Linda had to send her document to the printer on the third floor.

Linda had spent a lot of time in the Young Building over the course of her ten years teaching at the college, and she'd heard the stories. The third floor was said to be haunted. Although she was skeptical, she walked up the stairs slowly, the darkness closing in all around her.

Although the building was naturally dark most of the time, it seemed even darker that night.

The third-floor printer was in an alcove of the hallway, surrounded by office doors. The only sounds were Linda's footsteps, echoing throughout the hall, and the printer softly humming and whirring as it finished printing her document. She stood facing the printer, her back to the hall, waiting for it to finish so she could finally get out of there. That's when she felt something — something that chilled her to the bone. Someone was right behind her, breathing down her neck.

Linda spun around expecting to come face to face with whoever meant her harm, but the hallway was empty. None of the doors were open, so there was nowhere anyone could hide, and she could feel no draft that might explain the breathing sensation on her neck. She grabbed her printout, raced back downstairs to her office, gathered whatever personal belongings she couldn't leave behind, and bolted from the building. She was not only scared — she was also no longer a skeptic. The stories were true. The Young Building was haunted.

Another instructor, Lisa, had an odd and terrifying experience in the same hallway. It was early one winter morning and the sun hadn't risen yet. The world outside was pitch black. Lisa had arrived to work early to prepare for the day and was walking to her office. She caught sight of a colleague's reflection in a window at the end of the hall. He was creeping up behind her, arms outstretched like a monster in an old horror movie. The comical way he was walking was so over-the-top that Lisa couldn't help but laugh.

"I can totally see you!" she said, still watching his reflection approach her. She put her hands on her hips, pretending to be angry and sending a clear message to her prankster friend: *Busted!*

He took a few more steps until he was directly behind her, raised his hands even higher, and then he . . . disappeared.

He didn't just disappear — he *melted.* To Lisa's eyes, it had looked like he was made of paint and someone dumped a bucket of water over his head. She spun around and confirmed that she was alone.

The next time she saw her friend he was fine, and it was clear whatever presence had tracked her down in the hallway hadn't been human. Lisa believed it to be the resident ghost, but she had no idea how it had taken on her friend's appearance.

The Young Building originally opened in 1915 as the Victoria Normal School, the first teachers' college in the city. In the 1940s it was repurposed as a military hospital for wounded veterans returning home from World War II, and in 1970 Camosun College was founded and took over the building. It's possible the ghost is a former student or teacher. It's possible the ghost is a veteran who died in the building. It's also possible that there isn't only one ghost haunting the halls, but many. There's plenty of unexplained activity in the Young Building.

At one time the Camosun College radio station broadcast from the building, and it was an all-too-common occurrence to have pre-taped recordings ruined thanks to the spirits. Students were quite often puzzled and scared when they would listen to their recordings and hear voices other than their own, sometimes in a soft whisper, other times in animated conversation. Likewise, students creating videos for their school projects have often experienced the same troubling phenomenon.

The Young Building in 1915, when it was the Victoria Normal School

Meanwhile, senior photography students warn junior students about one of the building's darkrooms. Time after time, when a student sets up at a particular station to develop their photographs, they discover the magnifier has gone missing. After searching the darkroom for the missing item in vain, they often find the magnifier has returned to the station on its own.

Several custodians have reported unusual and disturbing events in the building. Norm, a man who had worked there a long time, was buffing the floors of the infamous third-floor hallway in the middle of the night. Suddenly the doors on both sides of the hall slammed shut at the same time. By nature Norm wasn't easily frightened, but he immediately turned off his buffing machine and went downstairs in search of a different task in a decidedly less creepy part of the building.

Campus security guards have also reported more than their fair share of ghost encounters. Alan had only worked for the college for one year when he received an alarm at 3 a.m. signifying that a motion sensor had gone off in the Young Building. Ever since Alan had been informed that the basement had served as a morgue when the building had been a hospital, he felt uneasy late at night on his own. But thanks to the alarm it couldn't be avoided. Taking a deep breath and building up his courage, Alan decided he'd start on the third floor and work his way down. The third floor, where so many others had had paranormal encounters, was empty. The second and first floors were empty as well. So Alan ventured into the basement. The hallway was well lit from ceiling lights running its length, but despite not being able to see anyone, Alan immediately felt certain that he wasn't alone. He also had a feeling that the unseen presence wasn't friendly.

"I'm not here to harm you," Alan said. "I just need to check the building."

The ghost didn't care about Alan's wants and needs. The light at the far end of the hall suddenly shut off, then the next light and the next and the next, creating a wall of darkness that was coming straight for him. Alan turned and fled from the building, never to return.

Another guard, Christine, had two terrifying experiences while working there. One night she heard muffled voices and stomping feet coming from the elevator. There shouldn't have been anyone in the building, and the people in the elevator were clearly fooling around, so she pressed the button to call the elevator down to her. As the elevator travelled from the third floor, the sounds got louder and louder and louder, until the elevator reached the ground floor. The doors opened and the commotion immediately died. Christine was shocked to discover the elevator was empty.

Another day Christine was training a new guard, showing her around campus. The new guard asked if they could go all the way to the top of the Young Building's clock tower. Christine wasn't thrilled by the prospect — construction crews were renovating it and the safety railings on the roof had been temporarily removed — but the young woman was so excited and hopeful that Christine eventually agreed. They climbed up the access ladder and Christine warned the new guard several times to be careful — one misstep and she would fall to her death.

Ironically, Christine slipped as she took her first step onto the roof. She fell forwards, helpless to save herself from plummeting over the edge of the building. But the young guard acted fast, grabbing the back of Christine's jacket and pulling her to safety. Christine took a moment to catch her breath and steady her nerves, then turned to thank the new guard for saving her life. But the new guard was still climbing up the ladder, completely unaware of how close to death Christine had come. If she hadn't saved Christine, who had?

Terrified, Christine informed the new guard that they were going back down to safety immediately. The new guard could tell by Christine's tone that she was serious. Without complaint, she headed straight back down the ladder. Before Christine followed, she turned back to the open air and said, "Thanks, Casper."

Christine was lucky it had been a friendly ghost on the roof that day. Most days in the Young Building, it isn't.

AN ETERNITY IN THE RED HOUSE

Calgary, Alberta

During a banquet at Rouge Restaurant, one of Calgary's most celebrated eateries, a hostess noticed a man sitting alone in an otherwise empty dining room. The man was old, dressed in a formal suit, and seated by the fire. They locked eyes for a moment, and before the hostess could say anything he suddenly stood up.

The hostess took a step back and suppressed a scream. The old man was transparent. He rushed toward her, flickering in and out of sight. She fled and found Chef Paul Rogalski, one of the restaurant's owners. As shocking as her account was, he wasn't surprised. He didn't believe in ghosts when he purchased Rouge Restaurant, but he believed in them after two years there.

Paul and the hostess returned to the dining room, but the old man was gone. The room was completely empty. They turned to leave, but before they did, one of the doors slowly swung open on its own.

Built in 1891, Rouge Restaurant was originally a private residence owned by Alfred and Helen Cross. Now designated as a Calgary Municipal and Alberta Provincial Heritage Site, the Cross residence is one of the city's oldest homes and features many unique architectural elements such as a hip roof, a widow's walk balustrade, and gingerbread trim. One of its most striking features is its brownish-red exterior, the colour of dried blood.

Alfred was a wealthy rancher, brewer and entrepreneur. He owned one of Alberta's largest ranches, founded the Calgary Brewing and Malting Company in 1892 and was one of the original founders of the Calgary Stampede in 1912. But the family's good fortune took a turn for the worse when three of their seven children contracted diphtheria. One day Alfred travelled to the train station to await the delivery of medicine he had ordered from Winnipeg. Sadly, Alfred was still waiting at the train station when two of the children, Nellie and Lizzie, died.

It's believed that they haunted the house after their deaths, and that their parents also remained in the house after they died to continue looking after their children's spirits. The old man the hostess saw was likely the ghost of Alfred.

On at least two different occasions, Chef Paul has seen a pan slide across the kitchen grill to the floor with a clatter. Others have heard footsteps running through empty hallways and strange laughter coming from the basement. Many have seen a woman in white, believed to be Helen, floating down the stairs. Sometimes servers hear furniture sliding across the floor above. When they go to investigate, one of Helen's chairs has been dragged across her bedroom to face the window. It's as if she's eternally waiting for a miracle.

The residence of Alfred E. Cross

One day a waiter had a terrifying experience. He was preparing for a banquet when he heard a young girl laughing in one of the dining rooms. He crept through the hallway, but the dining room was empty. Again he heard the laughter, coming from a different part of the restaurant. He followed the sound again, but every time he thought he was close, the laughter suddenly rang out from a different part of the restaurant. The waiter began to feel like he had been tricked into playing a game of tag, and that he was it. But who was he playing with? And where were they hiding?

The laughter floated down the stairs to the basement, and the waiter followed.

After searching the dark corridors, he came upon the walk-in freezer. It was open. Standing in the entrance was a young girl dressed in old-fashioned clothing. She laughed again and ran into the freezer, out of sight. The waiter feared for her safety. She shouldn't have been down there, and he had to make sure she got out safely. He rushed in after her but was shocked to find she had disappeared.

Suddenly the door slammed shut. The waiter tried to open it, but he was locked in. The girl was a ghost, and she had led him there as some sort of sick joke. He banged on the door and yelled, fearing for his life. If someone didn't come and let him out soon, his body temperature would drop dangerously low. Luckily the door opened shortly thereafter, seemingly on its own, and the waiter escaped. But the ghost's "game" had sent a message: Not all the spirits in Rouge Restaurant could be trusted.

Fun and games, or life and death? The young ghost of Rouge Restaurant doesn't seem to know the difference.

LIBRARY OF THE DEAD

Thornhill, Ontario

It was a quiet afternoon in the Thornhill Village Library. There were only a few people in the small building, working and reading on a sunny but frigid day in March of 1972. Gene Gerry and his wife were enjoying a relaxing day touring a few libraries, borrowing a stack of reading material to see them through the final days of winter.

They split up, and Gene wandered into the children's section at the back of the building. He stopped and covered his mouth and nose. The room smelled strongly of skunk. Although he thought he was alone, he noticed a woman in an old rocking chair. If the offensive odour bothered her she didn't show it. Sunlight streamed through one of the icy windows and bathed her in a warm glow.

"John," the woman muttered. "John, John, John . . ."

There was no one else in the room, and certainly no one named John. Gene felt bad for the woman and turned to look for his wife. When he turned back, the rocking chair was empty. The woman had vanished into thin air.

His wife didn't believe that he had seen what he claimed to see, but Gene insisted that the woman hadn't been a figment of his imagination. He was so upset by his paranormal encounter that he wrote a letter to the local newspaper, which was published days later. "If you could find out if anyone has ever seen this lady," his letter read, "even one person, well, just let my wife know. Then I will be vindicated."

One person? Not a problem. Many people, both patrons and staff alike, have had chilling experiences with the library ghost over the years. Some staff have heard the chair rocking as they approach the children's area only to find it to be empty. Others have also heard a frail cough and twitching and shuffling coming from the unoccupied chair. They believe the woman enjoys staring out the window watching passersby.

But who is she? The prevailing theory is the ghost is a woman named Ellen Ramsden. When you enter the Thornhill Village Library, you pass two historical plaques near the main entrance, both bearing Ellen's name. The building was constructed in 1851 as Ellen's personal residence, but sadly she didn't get to enjoy it for long before passing away at the age of thirty-nine, leaving behind her husband, miller John Ramsden, and their infant son John. This explains why the ghost has been heard muttering the name John over and over, but is she calling for her husband or her son? Perhaps she's calling for both.

Following Ellen's death, the building was converted into a grocery store and then a veterinary office before being turned into a library in 1960. In 1978 the neoclassical style property was designated under the Ontario Heritage Act by the Town of Markham for its historical value. Little did they know how much history truly lives on in the library.

In addition to the rocking chair in the children's area, much of the activity has been reported in a second-floor room that used to be Ellen's bedroom. Many nights at closing time, staff hear someone walking to and fro on the second floor. Thinking they somehow missed a library patron as they closed up, they head upstairs to inform whoever is there that the library is closed and thcy need to leave . . . only to find the second floor empty. The sounds are thought to be Ellen getting ready for bed.

One night, as a staff member was cleaning a coffee pot on the main floor, the silence was suddenly broken by the sound of footsteps running above. That was odd, the woman thought, since thick carpet had been installed on the second floor recently, and no one had heard any footsteps since. What followed was odder still, as she heard the upstairs window shutters slam closed and open repeatedly, which was impossible since they were bolted open. She made her way upstairs timidly and found no one was there, but when she looked through the window she saw the front gate slowly swing open and closed, as if someone had just left the property.

The Thornhill Village Library

Like the gate, some have seen the front door open and close on its own, while others have heard books being shelved and furniture moving about in empty rooms. And once a clock began running backwards inexplicably. Several retired staff have heard a ghostly voice say "Goodbye," as they left the library at the end of their final shift.

And then there are the people who, like Gene, have seen the ghost with their own eyes. A senior staff member once spotted a young library page — someone whose primary responsibility is shelving returned books — behaving oddly. The page was looking up the stairs, shaking and pale, her eyes and mouth wide. The staff member asked the page what was wrong, jolting the young girl out of her state of shock. It took some time before she was able to speak, but when she did, she admitted that she had just seen the ghost of a woman dressed in old-fashioned clothing standing at the top of the stairs, peering down at her.

A different page was once organizing books on a cart when a woman flew past her in a great hurry. As the woman rushed down the hall, her body became translucent until she disappeared completely from sight.

Many library patrons have reported to staff that when they walk past the building late at night, they have seen a woman in one of the second-floor windows watching them with a distant and forlorn look.

The Thornhill Village Library is filled with ghost stories. Some are in books, others are in the very walls.

THE BLOODY-NECK MAN

Myrnam, Alberta

The six-year-old girl woke in the middle of the night and screamed, a blood-curdling sound that could be heard throughout Fort de l'Isle, a small island in the North Saskatchewan River. Someone was standing in the shadows of her room, watching her. She took one terrified look at the intruder and knew. The Bloody-Neck Man had returned.

A few days earlier, her father, James King, had left their small home on the island for work. It was 1802 and James was employed by the North West Company as a clerk and fur trader. The first fort on the island of Fort de l'Isle was originally constructed in 1799 for the XY Company in order to compete for trade with the

Hudson's Bay Company and North West Company, both of which already had established forts farther south along the river. But by the end of 1801, both competitors had moved their operations north to the same island as the XY Company, creating the unique situation wherein three rival companies shared the same small footprint. The three companies had tried to find a way to peacefully coexist, but the fur trade was a dangerous business, and fights between the clerks were commonplace. It was a hard job suited for tough people, many of whom would stop at nothing to be successful.

Before being sent out on his latest job, James was warned that Joseph-Maurice LaMothe, a fur trader working for the XY Company, was interested in purchasing the very same furs James was after. James was assured that Joseph-Maurice would do whatever it took to get them.

Despite the warning, James wasn't concerned. He was big and strong and had dealt with no shortage of competitors over the years. He was confident he'd be able to handle himself against Joseph-Maurice. After all, Joseph-Maurice no longer had the element of surprise in his favour. To further protect himself, James arranged to travel *with* Joseph-Maurice.

Outside his home, James said goodbye to his wife and daughter, reassuring them that he would only be gone for three short days. He lifted his daughter off the ground and gave her a tight squeeze and a kiss.

"Please don't go," the girl said, staring deep into her father's eyes. She never liked it when he left, but for some reason she was especially out of sorts that day.

"Don't you worry none," James said as he handed his daughter to his wife. "Be a good girl and I'll be back before you know it." He said a final goodbye and left, leaving his family and Fort de l'Isle behind.

The girl was still upset the next day, but her mother was able to calm her down. However, she was completely distraught the second day and nothing her mother said made her feel better. Her mother couldn't understand what had gotten into her — they were accustomed to James being away for days on end, so she couldn't fathom why her daughter was so upset by his absence this time.

That night around midnight, the girl woke up. She wasn't alone. There was a man in her room standing beside the bed. A man with a bloody neck. The girl wanted to scream but didn't have time before he disappeared. And when she was alone, she realized she knew the Bloody-Neck Man. He was her father.

But how was that possible? He was away for work, and he hadn't smiled or hugged her. Instead he had looked sad, distant and full of regret. And his neck was smeared with blood and he had disappeared into thin air.

But she knew it had been him. She would recognize her father anywhere — especially his eyes. She called for her mother and tried to explain what had happened, but her mother told her it had only been a bad dream, and that her father would be fine. After some time, the girl finally drifted back into an uneasy sleep.

The next night it happened again. The girl woke around midnight and discovered she wasn't alone. The Bloody-Neck Man — her father — had returned. He didn't smile.

He didn't speak. He didn't even move. But his eyes were full of sorrow. Then blood gushed from his throat. His neck was wounded — the girl could see that now. He vanished and the girl called for her mother.

Her mother ran her fingers through her hair and promised her that everything would be fine. It was odd that her daughter had the same vision two nights in a row. What if something had happened to her husband? What if her daughter's night terrors were more than a nightmare? What if they were an omen?

She shook her head. That was foolish. James would return home the next day.

But when James did not return, his wife's concerns doubled. At first she blamed his tardiness on the bad weather. But when the weather improved and there was still no sign of James, she finally shared her fears with others on the island. Everyone tried to reassure her that the girl's dreams were just that — dreams — and that all would end well soon.

Finally James returned home. But instead of walking on his own two feet, his cold corpse was dragged by a couple of exhausted junior clerks. His wife and daughter were hysterical with grief. No one could console them, not for many days. The story of what had happened to James spread throughout the island — then along the Rocky Mountains — like wildfire.

On the day James and Joseph-Maurice set out from Fort de l'Isle, accompanied by two or three junior fur traders, the mood was upbeat. If either of the two experienced fur traders was uneasy being in the company of the other, neither showed it. The group travelled by dog-sled and snowshoes and arrived later that day at their destination, an Indigenous camp. Tired from the journey, they went to sleep straight away but rose early the next morning to get to work. Both James and Joseph-Maurice traded separately, and James was promised some beaver pelts that were in a nearby tent. When James went to retrieve them, he was told Joseph-Maurice had already taken them, and he was furious.

When the two men confronted one another, Joseph-Maurice asked if James would give the beaver pelts up if the tables were turned.

"I would not!" James barked.

Hearing the commotion, a crowd gathered.

Joseph-Maurice laughed bitterly. "So you do not get these, my friend."

The two men had journeyed together peacefully, but they had now entered a standoff. The victor would be the man who returned to Fort de l'Isle with the most furs — that was all that mattered. James grimaced and eyed the beaver pelts.

"Be careful," Joseph-Maurice said, his voice a low growl. "Do not force me."

For James, that was the last straw. He wouldn't stand to be intimidated. He reached for the beaver pelts.

Joseph-Maurice wouldn't stand by and let his competitor best him. He acted on instinct, raising his rifle and firing. The bullet tore a hole through James's throat. He fell to the ground, dead on impact. Upon realizing what he had done, Joseph-Maurice's tough demeanour instantly crumbled. Full of remorse, he blamed what he had done on the life he led. He had no choice. Taking and protecting one's furs, using force when necessary, was part of the job. Instead of trying to run and hide, Joseph-Maurice did the honourable thing and travelled east to turn himself in to the authorities and stand trial for his actions. As Fort de l'Isle was beyond the borders of Upper and Lower Canada, it was determined that a Canadian jury could not rule on the case, and Joseph-Maurice was set free. The resulting controversy of this decision led to the enactment of the Canada Jurisdiction Act in 1803, giving courts jurisdiction over crimes committed outside of Upper and Lower Canada.

When James's body was returned home, his wife knew their daughter's vision hadn't been a bad dream. James's ghost had appeared beside his daughter's bed the night he had died and the following night as well. For as long as she lived, his daughter couldn't forget how sorry her father had looked. Sorry he hadn't heeded the warning that Joseph-Maurice would stop at nothing to best him, sorry he had fought over something as trivial as a few extra beaver pelts, but most of all sorry that he couldn't hug his daughter and kiss his wife one final time.

RED EYES WATCHING YOU

Glovertown, Newfoundland and Labrador

Brandon was enjoying a leisurely stroll with his three-year-old daughter. They were walking along a wooded trail near their home in Glovertown, enjoying the crisp weather and the peaceful sights and sounds of the forest. All was well until Brandon's daughter spotted the Terra Nova Sulphite Mill, more commonly known as the Glovertown Pulp Mill, a commanding cement structure looming over the small community. The girl began to cry.

Brandon scanned the woods. There was nothing he could see that might have frightened her, so he asked what was wrong.

The girl didn't answer and asked to turn around. With a bad feeling forming in his gut, Brandon asked why. She said she wanted to go home. Again he asked her why, despite now having a pretty good idea what had caused his daughter's distress. Finally, pointing a trembling finger at the mill, she gave her answer. She didn't want to go any farther. The mill was, she said in a hushed tone, a "scary place."

It was as Brandon suspected. Shivers raced up and down his spine. He knew the mill was a scary place, but how did his daughter? She was only three. She couldn't possibly have heard the stories. But Brandon knew them all too well.

The incomplete Terra Nova Sulphite Mill

In the fall of 1921, construction on the mill came to a screeching halt. The mill had only processed one shipment of logs when the Norwegian investors had been hit with financial difficulties and ran out of money. The owners, the Terra Nova Sulphite Company, tried to secure a loan from the provincial government to complete construction but were unsuccessful. The partially completed mill sat vacant for two years before the Anglo-Newfoundland Development Company purchased it and shipped some wood to test its operation. Despite paying approximately $2 million for the property (roughly $30 million in today's money) the mill was determined to be too small for their needs, so the building sat empty once more. This time it was abandoned permanently, and it was determined that it would be too expensive to tear down the 35-metre-tall structure. So it sat, silent and still, like a concrete giant hibernating in the woods.

But rumours began spreading through Glovertown, as swift and chilly as winter wind through snow-capped trees. The locals began to speculate that the mill hadn't been completed on account of several tragedies that had plagued its construction. It was, they said, cursed.

In the summer of 1921, it was rumoured that one of the construction workers, a man named Sam, was sitting on the sandy shore of the Terra Nova River with his wife while their daughter swam in the water. The sun was setting on the horizon, and it was getting a little hard to see, so Sam warned his daughter not to go too far out. She agreed, laughing innocently, but continued to swim out farther from her parents. The girl's mother caught a chill as she sketched a drawing of the scenery and asked her husband to go to their small house nearby to fetch some warm clothing for their daughter. Sam hurried to their house, grabbed a sweater, and started back to his family. Screams cut through the peaceful evening.

He found his wife, who was unable to swim, sobbing hysterically on the shore. Their daughter was far from shore, bobbing up and down in the fast current, struggling to keep her head above water. Sam rushed into the river and swam as fast as he could, but he was too late. His daughter disappeared below the surface and didn't return. Sam dove underwater to try to rescue her, but sadly, he didn't return either. Father and daughter drowned together.

Construction on the mill was paused for a few days so the workers could grieve for their friend and his daughter. Once work resumed, strange things began happening in the mill. Construction equipment fell from the upper levels of the building, crashing down to the ground and narrowly missing people below. The workers assumed that the equipment must have been accidentally tipped over, but oddly there was never anyone above when items fell.

Later that year one of the supervisors was inspecting the morning's work when he heard someone crying in an unlit, unfinished part of the mill. It was lunchtime and most everyone was already eating outside while enjoying the fresh air, so the supervisor told the last few members of his crew that he would investigate the sound while they took their break.

A moment later the workers outside heard an earsplitting scream from inside the mill. They rushed in too late. The supervisor was dead, his body sprawled on the ground where they had heard the crying. The cause of his death was never determined.

During the following weeks more falling equipment narrowly avoided workers, and the disembodied crying was heard regularly throughout the building. Then, that fall, the most sinister event yet happened. A young worker named Mike and a co-worker were on one of the upper levels wrapping up their workday, when Mike caught sight of something peculiar in the distance: two points of red light. At first, he thought it was the reflection of the setting sun on a nearby tower. When he looked closer, he realized it wasn't the sun, but a pair of bright red eyes staring at him. Mike told his friend what he saw and pointed at the eyes. His friend took a quick glance, saw nothing, and told Mike he was being silly. However Mike was drawn toward the red eyes like a moth to a flame. As if in a trance, he left his friend behind and walked toward the tower. His co-worker noticed Mike was missing a moment later and looked up just in time to see a ghostly figure push Mike over the edge of the building. Mike plummeted to his death. The upper floors were searched thoroughly but there was no sign that anyone other than Mike and his co-worker had been up there at the time of the accident.

All these stories and more came rushing back to Brandon when his daughter refused to go anywhere near the "scary place." He remembered spending many weekends at the mill as a teenager, hanging out with friends. But one memory haunted him more than any other. He recalled one of the last times he and his friends had hung out at the mill — as he was leaving he heard a scream from behind. He spun around to see who was in distress, but none of his friends were behind him. Instead he saw a pair of red eyes glowing in the night, staring down at him from the mill's tower.

Today the incomplete Terra Nova Sulphite Mill remains in remarkably good shape despite being completely neglected for a century. Time will tell how long that will remain, but it's hard to imagine the town of Glovertown without the steel beams and cement rising over the treetops on the bank of the Terra Nova River. Venture near and you might see something terrifying that you can't explain. That is, if you don't heed the graffiti warning that recently appeared on one of the mill's walls:

RED EYES

I AM WATCHING YOU

DON'T FREAK OUT

Brampton, Ontario

Ishta Mercurio was on an informal tour of Peel's Art Gallery, Museum and Archives (also known as PAMA) when she first learned the building was haunted. It was August 2007, and she had signed up for a night class on acting. The sun outside was beginning to set, casting long shadows across the property, and there were only three or four people with Ishta at the time, making the tour intimate and a little extra creepy.

"If we're ever in the middle of the class and you hear weird noises," Kristine Marchese, the acting teacher who was leading the tour said, "or if you notice something, like a trap door was closed and now it's open, don't freak out."

There was a smattering of nervous laughter. Some of the students were clearly a little uncomfortable with the notion that they were about to spend the next few months studying in the company of restless spirits, but not Ishta.

I hope I get to see the ghost one day, she thought as a frisson of excitement raced up and down her spine.

Kristine went on to share some of the building's history. It was built in 1866 and originally served as the Peel County Courthouse. The following year, the Peel County Jail was built behind the courthouse. When it first opened, the jailhouse didn't have electricity or running water. Inmates slept on straw mattresses, and it often had more than sixty people crammed into its sixteen small cells. Three executions — all hangings — took place on the premises, one in 1909 and two in the 1940s. That year, Stefan Swyryda was accused and convicted of the murder of a teen boy. Both Stefan and his wife, Anna, maintained Stefan's innocence throughout his trial.

With all the talk of ghosts and hangings, Ishta felt compelled to look up. She noticed a shadowy area that was higher than the rest of the ceiling, and she couldn't help but wonder if that was the exact spot where Stefan and the others had been hanged.

It was said Anna was the most commonly spotted ghost, and that she was often seen wandering past the windows, crying for her husband and insisting that he was innocent. From that day on, Ishta stared at the windows closely every time she passed outside but saw nothing unusual, so she felt like her hope to see a ghost might never materialize.

Months passed, then a year. Ishta loved every moment of the acting class. She had studied acting at Bard College at Simon's Rock in Great Barrington, Massachusetts, before moving to Canada with her husband and settling in Brampton. They had two children four years apart. With one child in kindergarten and the other a toddler at home, it felt great do something just for her, exercising her acting muscles for the first time in years. Then one day, Kristine announced to the class that she had been researching the history of the old courthouse and had decided to write a play based on the case of Stefan Swyryda. It was to be called *A Complex Verdict*, and while they would need to hold auditions to cast many of the parts, Kristine asked Ishta if she would play the part of Stefan's wife, Anna.

"Yes!" Ishta exclaimed without a second's hesitation. She had signed up for the class hoping for the opportunity to perform before an audience once more, and she immediately began envisioning her part. If she wouldn't get to see the ghost of Anna, she'd get to embody Anna's spirit, and that was a far more gratifying prospect.

She wasted no time getting to work. Stefan and Anna were Polish immigrants, so Ishta recruited her mother's neighbour, who was Polish, to help her work on her accent. They also wrote a few lines of dialogue together since the play was being performed in a uniquely immersive fashion. Some of the performers had no script and wouldn't even be "on stage." Instead, the play was to be performed over several nights in the actual courthouse where Stefan had been convicted, with Ishta and some of the cast seated among the audience in the public gallery. Next Ishta made some alterations to a period costume she had kept from an eighth-grade school project to match the look and style of a Polish immigrant in the early 1900s. And naturally she spent a great deal of time rehearsing in the old courthouse with the rest of the cast.

The sun had set on a cold winter night when, during a break, one of the actors suggested they dim the lights and take pictures of the courtroom. Maybe — just maybe — they'd capture the image of a ghost. The air felt a little heavier that evening, as if there was an unseen presence presiding over the rehearsals. Ishta had begun to feel the weight of bringing a real person to life and wanted to do Anna justice, so the thought of doing something as lighthearted as taking a few pictures in search of ghosts was a welcome break. After all, a small part of her still hoped to leave the play with a bevy of new acting skills and a ghost sighting under her belt.

The actors took out their phones and began photographing the room. It was quiet — deathly quiet — and the heavy sensation in the air grew even heavier. Ishta felt a ghostly presence in the room. And then when she looked closely at the pictures they had taken, she was completely stunned.

Wow, Ishta thought, her excitement reaching new heights. *They're here.*

There were blue, translucent orbs hovering in the air of every picture. They reminded Ishta of the bubble that Glinda, the Good Witch travels in in *The Wizard of Oz.*

There was little doubt among the group that they had captured ghost orbs in their pictures.

Looking around the courtroom, feeling like she was surrounded by spirits she couldn't see with the naked eye, Ishta didn't feel frightened or intimidated. Instead she believed the ghosts were happy that their story was being told and Stefan and Anna were being vindicated after nearly a century of injustice. But some of the other actors were creeped out by both the pictures and the general vibe in the room, and they weren't too disappointed when Kristine walked in and broke up the amateur ghost hunting experiment.

"Get over the ghost stuff, guys," she said. "We have a show to put on!"

The actors put away their phones — some reluctantly, some relieved — and carried on with the evening's rehearsals. Ishta didn't see the ghosts again . . . at least, not in the PAMA.

One week before opening night, bright and early in the morning, Ishta was home in her kitchen preparing breakfast for her two-year-old son, Carter. She lived about a fifteen-minute walk from PAMA. Her husband was at work and her older son was at school, so she and Carter were alone. With the Polish phrases she had practised running through her head, Ishta took a bowl of Cheerios to her son in his highchair beside the kitchen table.

"Look," Carter said, pointing behind his mother. "A lady!"

I'm a lady, Ishta thought. *But he's not pointing at me . . .*

"Do you mean me?" she asked, just in case.

"No, lady," he said, pointing more deliberately over his mother's shoulder.

Thinking he must have been pointing at a woman outside, Ishta turned around slowly and looked out the kitchen window. There was no one there.

"Outside you can see a lady?" she asked.

"No, kitchen!" he answered with a smile.

Ishta placed the bowl of Cheerios down and said, "In the kitchen?" She began to feel a presence behind her.

"Lady!" Carter said.

Ishta felt her skin tighten and the hair on her arms stand on end. Without a shadow of a doubt, Ishta knew they were not alone. *My son can see a ghost*, she thought. Wanting to know what the ghost lady looked like, she asked, "Is the lady wearing a dress, or is she wearing pants, like Mommy?"

"Dress."

This is her, Ishta thought, picturing Anna. *She followed me home.*

Carter's eyes went wide, and he watched the ghost walk out from behind Ishta's back, through the kitchen, and down the front hall.

"There go lady," he said, then cheerfully stuck a Cheerio in his mouth as if nothing unusual or alarming had just taken place.

Unusual? Certainly. But alarming? Ishta didn't feel that way. Deep down in her bones she believed that Anna had visited her home to get a better sense of what type of person Ishta was. Ishta was overcome by a calm and peaceful feeling, reassuring her that Anna had given her permission to tell her story in the play. It felt like a gift.

At rehearsals that night, Ishta told the others what had happened that morning. Some straight up didn't believe her, but others did, claiming that kids have a keener perception than adults for seeing ghosts. Ishta agreed, and it was a little creepier being in the old courthouse now that she knew the ghost stories were *really* real.

Opening night finally arrived. The building was filled with nervous energy and the hustle and bustle of cast and crew rushing through their final preparations. The audience entered the courthouse and took their seats. As soon as the show began, something changed. A heavy quiet descended upon the room. The air felt charged, like there were more people in the courtroom than those that were visible. Ishta felt Anna's presence more strongly than ever before, which calmed the butterflies in Ishta's stomach and filled her with confidence. She felt like she had Anna's final permission to bring her to life, or back to life, in a manner of speaking. The play was a great success and when the show ended, most of the audience gave the performers a standing ovation — the rest gave a floating ovation.

Ishta went on to be a children's author, writing *Bite Into Bloodsuckers* (co-written with Kari-Lynn Winters) and *Small World.* But she never forgot the paranormal encounters she experienced as a result of the acting class she took at PAMA. It's been said that acting should be larger than life. Sometimes acting also needs to be larger than the afterlife.

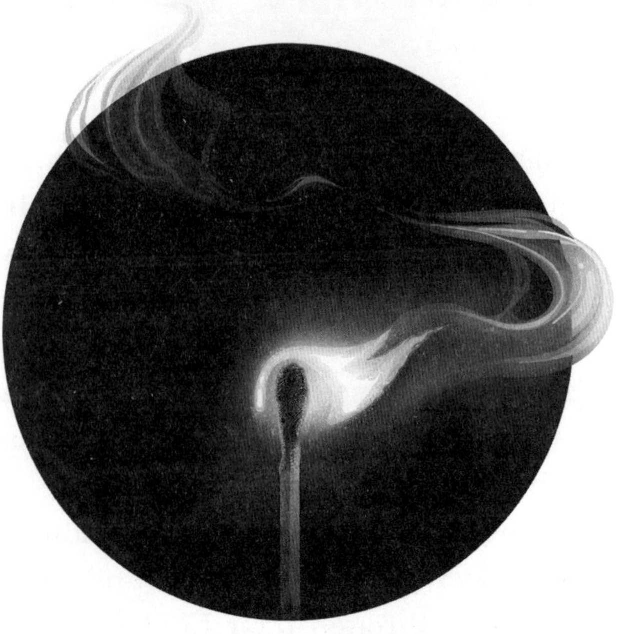

NO REST FOR THE WEARY

Cascade, British Columbia

It's safe to assume that the man who preferred to go simply by the name Mr. L. had not watched many horror films in his life. For if he had, it's unlikely he would have agreed to spend a night alone in an abandoned house in the middle of the wilderness. But in June 1961, that's exactly what he did.

Mr. L. was driving from Vancouver to Calgary along the Crowsnest Highway when he spotted a car pulled off to the side in the distance. He saw a man trying to figure out what was wrong with the vehicle, and as he got closer, he had a startling realization. The man was an old friend whom he hadn't seen in a long time. Shocked by the chance encounter, Mr. L. pulled over to see if he could help. His friend hopped into the car for a ride to the nearby city of Grand Forks so they could arrange to have a tow truck return for the broken-down vehicle.

As they caught up, the friend happened to mention an abandoned house a little past Grand Forks near Cascade, a boom town founded in 1896 that had become a ghost town by 1950. And speaking of ghosts, the friend said the house was haunted — far too haunted and terrifying for anyone to ever spend the night.

Cascade, British Columbia

But Mr. L. was quick to rise to challenges and wasn't afraid of ghosts. Half jokingly, the friend said he'd pay Mr. L. ten dollars if he could stay in the house overnight. Mr. L. was feeling brave and, since he didn't have anywhere else he needed to be that night, accepted the bet. They shook on it, and the friend showed him the way.

At first glance, Mr. L. couldn't help but laugh. Staying in the house was going to be the easiest ten dollars he'd ever earned. Situated on the top of a hill with a picturesque creek beside it, the two-storey house and surrounding woods were a beautiful sight to behold. Sure, the house was a little rundown and clearly hadn't been lived in for some time, and yes, it was a little creepy looking, but that didn't matter. Mr. L. was planning on going to bed early and sleeping through until morning. He grabbed his bag and some sandwiches he'd bought on the road and got out of the car. His friend said farewell and promised he'd be back to pick him up bright and early the next morning, then drove off in Mr. L.'s car, backtracking to Grand Forks so he could hire a tow truck driver.

Other than the gentle whoosh of the breeze, the chirps of the birds perched in the surrounding trees and the steady buzz of insects, everything was silent. It was a little eerie, and Mr. L. found himself thinking of an Alberta ghost town he was familiar with: Frank. In 1903 a massive rockslide buried most of the town and killed more than ninety of the six hundred residents. Many believe Frank is haunted by the souls of the unfortunate people who died in the slide, and Mr. L. couldn't help but wonder what Cascade used to be like.

Cascade didn't live long, largely because of two large fires that broke out in 1899 and 1901. One man died when he rushed into a hotel to save others trapped within. All buildings were abandoned or demolished by the 1970s, leaving behind a small cemetery and the spirits of the people who once called the town home.

Night was falling as Mr. L. explored the house. He was happy to discover it was still partially furnished, putting to bed any concerns that he might need to sleep on the floor. He decided to sleep in a room with a nice view facing south. He laid down and stared at the full moon through his window as he drifted off. Coyotes howled and whined in the distance. It was very peaceful, but he decided to lock the bedroom door — just in case. In case of what? Probably nothing, but locking the door gave Mr. L. a little peace of mind. He lay back down and stared once more at the moon, thinking of bets won and easy money.

Just before midnight, the bedroom door flew open and slammed against the wall with a nerve-shattering *slam.* Mr. L. flew out of bed and raced to the hallway. It was empty. He closed and locked the door again. For good measure he slid a large dresser in front of it. Feeling only marginally better, he went back to bed.

Thwack! Thwack! Thwack!

It was the sound of someone splitting logs outside his window. Who would be chopping wood in the middle of the night, not to mention in the middle of nowhere? Mr. L. looked through the window but couldn't see anyone, so he went outside. He was alone, but there was an axe leaning against the side of the house and a small pile of split logs beside it. He thought back to when he'd first arrived and was pretty sure he had seen a pile of logs — not yet split — in that very spot, but he must have been mistaken. Still, he figured it wouldn't hurt to take the axe inside, so he picked it up and returned to his bedroom.

Shortly after he laid back down with the axe clutched

tightly in his hands, the sound of someone splitting wood resumed. He waited in bed for as long as his nerves could take it, but eventually he rushed downstairs to catch whoever was creating the disturbance. He barged through the front door but still didn't see a soul, and now all the logs were split and stacked in a neat pile.

Mr. L. walked back inside and laughed. *If they want more work*, he thought, *they will have to cut more trees.*

The moment his head hit the pillow, he heard the rumble of a small engine starting up, the whirring of a saw and the crash of a tree falling in the bush. It was as if the ghosts had heard his thoughts and had taken him up on his challenge. Mr. L. rushed to the window and the sounds of falling trees stopped abruptly. He went back to bed, and the saw roared to life again.

Mr. L. lay there for hours listening to the sounds of saws and axes and crashing trees and wood being split. He was concerned that if anyone still lived nearby in the woods they would come to complain about the commotion, but no one did.

I will *try to sleep*, Mr. L. ordered himself. But then a new sound — coming from inside his room — joined the fray. Hissing and meowing and scratching and clawing, as if a cat fight had broken out beneath his bed. He struck a match, but someone unseen blew it out. He struck a second match, but it was blown out too. Giving up on the matches, he dragged the bed across the floor. There was nothing beneath it. When he laid back down, the bed began shaking violently, nearly tossing him to the floor. He stood up, and the bed fell still. He looked out the window, and the sounds of the woodcutters stopped.

"Okay, I will not sleep," Mr. L. said, noticing in his reflection that his eyes looked much wilder than usual. "But believe me, you are going to work!"

As if in answer, someone started pounding on the bedroom door. Thinking a passerby had finally heard the commotion and come to complain, Mr. L. dragged the dresser out of the way and pulled on the doorknob, but whoever was on the other side pulled back. After a momentary struggle, Mr. L. pulled with all his might. Whoever was on the other side suddenly let go, and Mr. L. fell backwards. A cold gust of air swept past him with a deep, guttural laugh.

It was 3 a.m. and Mr. L. was at his wits' end, so he slammed the door and raced back to bed. But the ghosts were not done tormenting him. Without any logical explanation he received an electrical shock and his body convulsed. He flew out of bed and sat wearily on a chair by the window, but a second later the chair was pulled out from under him and he fell, banging the back of his head on the floor. The same loud laughter filled the room.

Giving up any hope of falling asleep, Mr. L. stood by the window until the sun rose. The light gave him more courage than he had felt in hours, so he opened the bedroom door and stepped into the hall. There, in the middle of the floor, were his sandwiches, smashed to bits. It was like the ghosts were having one last laugh at his expense.

His friend pulled into the driveway shortly thereafter. Mr. L. accepted his ten-dollar reward. He'd earned it.

Photo credit: Colleen Morris

Joel A. Sutherland is an author and librarian. He is the author of several books in the Haunted Canada series, as well as *Be a Writing Superstar*, *Summer's End*, *Screamers* and Haunted, a series of middle grade horror novels. His short fiction has appeared in many anthologies and magazines, alongside the likes of Stephen King and Neil Gaiman. He has been a juror for the John Spray Mystery Award, the Monica Hughes Award for Science Fiction and Fantasy, the Amy Mathers Teen Book Award, and the TD Canadian Children's Literature Award.

He appeared as "The Barbarian Librarian" on the Canadian edition of the hit television show *Wipeout*, making it all the way to the third round and proving that librarians can be just as tough and goofy as anyone else.

Joel lives with his family in southeastern Ontario, where he is always on the lookout for ghosts.